PLAYFUL
BY DESIGN

Your **Stress-Free Guide** to Raising **Confident, Creative Kids** Through **Independent Play**

Myriam Sandler
creator of Mothercould

with Rachel Holtzman

HARPER
Celebrate

Cover design by Sabryna Lugge
Interior design by Jeffrey Jansen | Aesthetic Soup
Photography by Kris D'Amico and Nick Bumgardner with Reactor Media
Illustrations by Mat Edwards

ISBN 978-1-4002-4974-9 (HC)
ISBN 978-1-4002-4978-7 (epub)
ISBN 978-1-4002-4976-3 (audio)

Printed in Malaysia
25 26 27 28 29 PJM 5 4 3 2 1

For Nicole, Emma, and Ariana,
who gave me the courage to start,
the strength to continue,
and the passion to grow.
You are my "why."

Contents

A Better Way to Play

O ne of my favorite things I hear from people is, "It must be nice to be able to play with your kids all day." It makes sense that they'd think this—I am, after all, constantly sharing posts and videos of me filling recycled tissue boxes with rainbow-colored ice-pop sticks, whipping up batches of foamy hot-pink dish soap "love muffins," and demoing taste-safe playdough.

But this mama of three also works full-time, and as much as I love my kiddos (which is a lot), it's not all finger painting and dress-up 24/7. Our reality is much different than me playing with the kids all day, every day. For most of their free time, my girls play *independently*. And no, that's not code for me leaving them in a room with the TV on while I take Zoom meetings (though, no shame in that game when it's needed!). Rather, they're helping themselves to kid-friendly spaces in the house that are thoughtfully stocked with open-ended activities and materials that encourage curiosity, imagination, and, most important, self-direction. Because of that, the time I spend with them is so much more focused and intentional. They're happy, growing, and learning; I have a healthier balance of *mom*-me and *me*-me; and *everybody* wins. But before we dive into how we're going to do the same thing for you without spending a bunch of money on new toys or moving into a bigger home to accommodate one of these seemingly magical spaces of your own, let's back up slightly.

They're happy, growing, and learning; I have a healthier balance of *mom*-me and *me*-me; and *everybody* wins.

When I launched my online parenting and lifestyle platform seven years ago, it was with the core idea of helping moms find small parenting wins throughout the day, so they can have a little more *aaah* and a little less *AAARGH!* in their lives. After all, from the moment we start thinking about raising our children, we're inundated with unsolicited advice. We don't, however, get much in the way of realistic support, encouraging guidance, accessible tools, or even simple high fives.

When my eldest daughter was a baby, she had a sensory aversion to many foods, which made introducing solids an overwhelming and isolating challenge (a *vast* understatement). During my time working with kids with ADD and ADHD at Florida International University's Center for Children and Families while getting my bachelor's degree in psychology, I saw the therapeutic power of sensory play firsthand, and I realized that it could be one solution for acclimating her to different textures. It gave me the idea to introduce her to squishy-, slimy-, wet-, and

rough-feeling items through activities using things like water, playdough, grains, and even slime. This type of sensory play

This type of sensory play encourages learning through exploration and problem-solving while also building important neural connections in the brain that strengthen everything from language to motor skills.

encourages learning through exploration and problem-solving, while also building important neural connections in the brain that strengthen everything from language to motor skills.[1] Pretty amazing for just smooshing up some goo! It was such a lightbulb moment for our family, and I was desperate to connect with other parents who might be going through the same thing, so I decided to share our experience.

Most of all, I wanted to create a community that didn't just give mothers (and fathers, educators, and caregivers) some fun and inspiring resources, but I wanted to also offer a place where we could *celebrate* our victories. That's why I named this space Mother*could*, after that energizing, empowering feeling that I got from helping my own daughter, and that's how I want everyone to feel when they have a parenting win on their own terms—no matter how big or small.

So when I thought about what I wanted this book to offer readers, I came back to that central goal. How can I set up parents for more feel-good successes? And to that I say: with more play! But as I mentioned before, I'm not talking about more play for *you*. Rather, what I am talking about is equipping you to give your children the tools to unlock their creativity and encourage them to engage in kid-directed, kid-executed, and ultimately kid-enriching play, using the materials and spaces you already have in your house. Or what I like to call being *playful by design*.

It's Time to Get Comfortable with the B-Word

Somewhere along the way, parents got the memo that we needed to entertain our kids. All. The. Time.

I like to say that we've been taught to believe that we should be the *architects* of our children's play, while the kids are the

construction workers. Meaning, we come up with the plan and the kids execute it. But really, when it comes to activities that

build problem-solving skills, encourage social and academic development, nurture independence and self-expression, and help work through emotions, we need to flip those roles.

And if we're going to put kids in charge of their own entertainment, then we're also going to have to get comfortable with hearing that oh-so-fun phrase using the dreaded b-word: "I'm bored."

But *boredom* is not a bad word! In fact, boredom is where imagination is born. Like any other skill, it takes time to get the hang of self-directed, open-ended play. With time and nurturing (and lots of road-tested tips from me), it'll get easier for you *and* them! And eventually, you'll realize what a game-changer this new dynamic is for the entire household. For the parents, there's no more feeling overwhelmed and stretched thin by unrealistic expectations about how to entertain your children. And for your children, you're giving them the most beautiful gift: the ability to be independent self-starters who are in touch with their own creativity. In short, everyone will feel happier, more energized, more fulfilled, and, ultimately, more connected.

This is where *Playful by Design* comes in. These are thoughtful, dedicated, play-*enhancing* spaces. Or, in other words, they are:

- ▶ stocked with activities based on your children's ages and interests (and your tolerance for mess—I got you, neat freaks!)

- ▶ intuitively organized and easy for kids to navigate on their own

- ▶ easy to straighten up (and keep that way)

- ▶ nice to look at (because it's part of your home).

But let's get one thing straight: Creating an aesthetically pleasing, impeccably organized, fully immersive play space that looks like it came straight out of an Instagram feed does *not* mean buying more toys. And it definitely doesn't require giving up an entire room in your house.

On the contrary, these spaces call for:

Open-ended toys and activities

Translation: things that require your child to supply the creativity. The best part about open-ended activities is that they can often be made using recycled materials. Think cardboard boxes, toilet-paper rolls, bottle caps, and egg cartons. (Don't worry, I'll be giving you *lots* of inspo for what to do with all these things.)

Less stuff, not more

Ever notice the holiday/birthday effect, where tons of toys enter the house, but your child is already bored of them a week later? That's because choosing from too many toys can be overwhelming for kids and can ultimately take the shine off once-coveted playthings. Instead, I recommend following a *toy rotation*, something we'll be talking about in more detail on page 79. But basically, by making a small, curated selection of toys and activities available for a set period of time while the remainder is stored away, you'll not only spark new interest in their existing toys, but you'll also find yourself buying fewer toys each year.

A dedicated space

Any space. Truly! It could be an entire room or a tiny nook, a desk in a bedroom, a closet, a corner, or even a drawer. No matter the size of your home, there's a play space that can fit—and this book will cover them all.

Playful by Design is your blueprint for effortlessly designing, installing, and maintaining your own upgraded play spaces that seamlessly evolve as your children grow up. Each chapter is devoted to one of a range of different spaces that can be mixed and matched to suit any household—because having

A dedicated space

more than one dedicated play space in the home is often what best suits a family's natural rhythm and can help you better tailor them to your children and their interests (and grow along with them). The chapters that follow also reflect the many ways these spaces can look, depending on the ages of the children using them, their interests, and how much room there is to work with. And they include tons of suggestions for how to maximize the use of that space, insight into how you can mostly use what you already own, and tips for materials you may need.

But before you dig in, I'll walk you through the need-to-knows. This will include the psychology and benefits of independent play (for all members of the family), what independent play means—and what it doesn't. (No one's telling you to abandon your kid! And it doesn't have to involve paint or slime.) We'll also cover how to help your family transition to independent play. I'll give you plenty of talking points and prompts for how to help you set healthy boundaries and give your child or children a sense of ownership of the space as well as a secure sense of safety, how to talk to your kids about how exciting it is that they can make these choices for themselves, and how to reassure them that this does not mean Mommy and Daddy don't want to play. In fact, we'll discuss how when you do play, you can do it in a focused, mindful way. (I guarantee that you can put that phone down for ten minutes!) And last, I'll do my best to convince the whole family that it's not such a bad thing to make a mess every once in a while—and within reason.

Next, I'll take you through the play-space-planning process, which applies to any space or spaces you choose, and can be referenced over and over as your needs or home changes. This includes planning the space (reflecting on who is going to use it and what kind of play will happen there), decluttering (perhaps the most crucial part of this entire process—I promise I'll make it painless . . . and your kids will barely miss most of the items that go away!), and organizing toys by type (getting you closer to your toy-store-fantasy play space). But maybe most importantly, we'll also be talking through how to *maintain* the space, to keep it functional *and* engaging.

When you do play, you can do it in a focused, mindful way.

After you've become familiar with the foundational process, we'll jump into the play spaces themselves. Since each chapter will focus on a specific type of space—whether it's in a bedroom, outdoors, in the bath, on the go, tucked in a nook, or spread out over an entire room dedicated to play—that will allow us to dig even deeper into how to tailor your play space to your specific needs. And, to make sure you really get a sense of how to put all the pieces together, I'll include tons of sample rooms from which you can draw inspiration.

As for what comes next? Nothing but the good stuff (well, besides the inevitable tantrums, meltdowns, and other fun things we get to navigate as parents)—more time for your children to blossom and grow as creative and independent little people; more time to do the things you need and want to do; more peace of mind that you are, in fact, giving your children important tools they'll thank you for one day (probably); and more opportunities to feel the joy of all of the above. In short: a little more *aaah*.

Now, go play!

Myriam

The (Painless) Prep

PART 1

The Life-Bettering Magic of **Independent Play**

CHAPTER 1

P eople don't believe me when I tell them my girls are content to play on their own during some stretches of the day. It comes as a shock that I can devote time to getting work done, doing dishes, throwing in some laundry, reading a book (!)—whatever activity I need or want to be doing in that moment—and they will be in their dedicated play space, happily cooking up their own activities, games, and mini telenovelas, with little to no adult supervision. Oh, and did I mention that the girls are allowed to turn on the television or their tablets anytime they want (for preapproved apps and shows)? And that even after twenty or so minutes of watching TV or playing a video game, they actually *choose* to be in their play space instead? I have a feeling that even fewer of you believe me now! But I can assure you that this is all very real, involves zero brainwashing or bribery, and does not require me to have a homeschool license or spend my evenings planning how to make the next day fun and exciting. *It's simply the magic of independent play.*

While there was no magic wand involved (there never is!), this seemingly too-good-to-be-true scenario is the result of a very simple shift in our home. It all started when my husband, Marc, and I were living in a small, two-bedroom apartment with no closet space and an infant. Our daughter was the first grandchild on both sides of our very large family, so every holiday or visit resulted in her receiving a monsoon of toys. And we, being first-time parents, initially thought that she should be able to play with every single one. After all, kids love toys, right?!

And yet, do you think Nicky felt like she was in toy-store heaven, with everything she could possibly need and want at her infant and toddler fingertips? Not even close. The opposite was true: She was overwhelmed by having so many choices and often wouldn't engage with her toys because she couldn't figure out where to start. Or she'd pick one up, play for thirty seconds, then move on to the next, only to never return to the first. And *we* were overwhelmed because we couldn't figure out what to do with all this stuff that barely kept her interested.

She was overwhelmed by having so many choices and often wouldn't engage with her toys because she couldn't figure out where to start.

That's when I took things to the internet and read about toy rotations, or only setting out a portion of your toys while

storing the rest. The idea, which is by no means mine to own and has been used for many years all over the world, is that kids are inspired by having *fewer* choices of things to play with, not more. So I took about three-quarters of our toys and stored them anywhere I could. Now, instead of walking into her room and seeing huge baskets loaded up with stuffies (which she would just dump out and move on to the next thing—one of the reasons why you'll never see me recommend deep storage!), crates packed with toys (same reason), and a

bookshelf groaning with every single book she owned, she had a fraction of that, all clearly on display. *Instantly* she was more engaged.

The other shift was that I started noticing the difference between toys that flashed, made noises, and essentially did the play for my daughter, and those that required her to fill in those blanks. Again, as first-time parents, we thought when it came to toys, the flashier, the better. What better way to entertain your kid?! But as Nicky turned two years old, we could see how differently she interacted with these different items. The toys with all the bells and whistles tended be more of a novelty. (Not to mention the fact that they made us all feel a little overstimulated and cranky when they were on all the time.) But the blocks, magnetic tiles, and wooden ice cream set (that didn't have the clanging cash register and songs about scooping the perfect cone) seemed to hold her attention more. And they didn't just hold her attention—these "open-ended" toys seemed to stimulate her imagination. A lot. She wasn't passively being entertained; she was actively *playing*.

> She wasn't passively being entertained; she was actively *playing*.

At first I thought, *Wow, she's young to be able to entertain herself for twenty minutes*. But then I realized that that's exactly what we had set her up to be able to do. We'd spend much of our time playing together—mainly making activities out of things I needed to be doing around the house—but then for a few sweet, blissful stretches throughout the day, I'd let her explore her toys on her own. And the more I phased out potentially overstimulating toys, or made only a couple available at a time versus five, the more invested and creative she became with her open-ended activities.

At the same time, I started learning more about sensory play, or activities that stimulate the senses—touch, sight, hearing, smell, taste—as a possible solution for helping Nicky with a serious texture aversion to food. We spent time together in the kitchen making the recipes, such as a batch of taste-safe playdough or dyed rice, and then she'd enjoy a stretch of time playing with those materials while I made dinner or picked up the house. I loved that while we did these activities, we were also working on language by talking through the steps and chatting about colors or temperature or measurements, and practical motor skills such as scooping, pouring, and mixing. And she loved getting to make a (very reasonable) mess. Meanwhile, the projects typically used things I already had in the house or cost less than five dollars.

But what I maybe loved most of all—and I know you all will agree—was not having to put so much pressure on myself to come up with different ways to play. The more absorbed Nicky was with these simple activities and her toys—because I made them more accessible and appealing and had curated a selection that inspired endless play—the less coaching or prompting I had to do. And yet, I still had the peace of mind that she was working on important skills and developing in a healthy, beautiful way.

Fast-forward almost eight years, and Nicky's play has organically evolved with her, as well as with her two younger sisters. Now, instead of them constantly noodling around and telling me they're bored or they want to watch TV, they are happily playing in their playroom or bedrooms independently. Their toys and materials suit their current interests, and while it's true they can have their tablets whenever they want, they typically use the technology available to them to make up dances and skits. Because their tools for play are housed in shared spaces, they can play together (as they often do for *hours*). And when I throw a toy rotation into the mix—meaning, I replace some of their current toys with toys from storage and rearrange things on the shelves—you'd think it was Hanukkah all over again! Yet I haven't spent a single penny on anything new. (In fact, I've gotten rid of things.)

> I still had the peace of mind that she was . . . developing in a healthy, beautiful way.

What I can't express enough is that this is not unique to me and my family. My kids are not built any differently than yours. We, too, are sometimes just trying to get through the day, one mac-and-cheese dinner at a time. We are juggling hectic work schedules, after-school activities, homework, and housework with never enough hours in the day. But with a few tiny shifts in our physical space (fewer toys, thoughtfully arranged) and one huge shift in our mental one (that kids can and should play on their own), the magic happened. And we're going to do the same for you and your family.

What Independent Play Means to Me

▶ Creating small opportunities throughout the day for children to play with toys and materials that engage them.

▶ Instilling the ability for your child to look inward for entertainment versus outward (particularly to an adult).

▶ No longer being the gatekeepers of your child's play. No more *Can I paint? Can I take out the puzzles?* Your child knows exactly what they can do and how to do it. (And how to clean it up afterward.)

▶ Less pressure to be your child's primary schoolteacher, art instructor, occupational therapist, and speech pathologist.

- More peace of mind, because you know your child's play spaces are engaging, age appropriate, and safe.

- More peace in general, because no one is relying on you to track down the paper, scissors, LEGO bricks, and dress-up accessories.

- More independence as an adult to do what needs to be done around the home.

- Feeling more present, because you had the time in your day to tackle more of your to-do list.

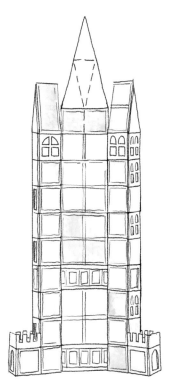

- Liberation from the seemingly endless task of cleaning up after your child, because they know where their toys go when they are done with them and are able to access those spaces themselves. (Sometimes with gentle prompting.)

- Feeling connected to your child, even when you're busy with another task or person.

- Going to bed feeling good about yourself as a parent, because you met your child's needs and didn't have to burn yourself out doing so.

The Life-Changing Magic
of Independent Play: Kids' Edition

Not only does independent play make your life a whole lot better, it's also amazing for your child. We've witnessed each of these benefits in our own family and Mothercould community:

It empowers children to be more independent

This transfers over to all areas of their lives, whether it's learning how to fill their own water glass, set the table, help with meal prep, or grab a towel, toilet paper, sunscreen, or other item when they need it.

It builds self-esteem

Playing independently allows kids to explore their environment at their own pace, become more self-sufficient, and problem-solve on their own, which all add up to feelings of positive self-worth.

It gives them a strong sense of self

Kids who craft their own play develop a deeper connection with themselves, which translates into wanting to form relationships with people because they truly like them and not just because they don't want to be by themselves.[2] Also, it equips kids for scenarios when their parent is not present or involved.

It gives them a sense of ownership

This translates into responsibility. And not just for their toys, but also for their other belongings and other spaces in the home, such as their bedrooms. It's a big shift from *my parents own this* to *I own this*, and it's a gift for kids to have a space they can control, feel responsible for, and be themselves in.

It's calming

Because kids can choose the amount of sensory input and stimulation they're getting from their play, they can meet their own needs and stay more even-keeled.[3]

It reinforces the family unit

They learn the idea that what we do in the home affects other people, and what they do affects us.

It builds real-life skills

Whether it's self-starting play, working collaboratively through an activity, using the resources around them in new and inventive ways, or navigating conflict with siblings or friends, we've observed time and time again in our home how independent play helps kids develop resilience, imagination, patience, persistence, and, of course, independence.

It encourages inclusivity and collaboration

Independent, open-ended play requires kids to work together to reinforce that play—and the more imaginations in the mix, the better. This strengthens the connections your child is making with their siblings or their peers, as well as the empathy and positive compromise that come from collaborative play.[4]

It exponentially expands play

When kids are the architects of their own play, the possibilities are limitless. They have an innate ability to see their toys and tools as so much more than what an adult with their fixed-state mentality might think of, and that child's imagination can run free when we're not interfering. Or as I like to think of it: Play begets play.

Making the Transition to Independent Play

This is a conversation with two parts: one for your child and one for you. The great news is that kids need little encouragement when it comes to playing without an adult—when they have access to a thoughtfully curated selection of open-ended toys and materials that interest them. And if you're following the steps in chapter 2, that's naturally available to them. Easy-peasy. Plus, if you're gradually exposing your child to this new skill—and it *is* a skill—over time they'll pick it up seamlessly.

For us parents, on the other hand, it's not quite as straightforward. To be clear, this process can feel energizing and liberating and have the most amazing payoff. But it requires a mental shift on your part. The way we set up our kids' play spaces is part of it, but the other big piece is how we're truly allowing our kids to become the leaders in their own play. I've listed some things for you to be thinking about, for both your child and you.

For You

Let go of control

You may not even realize you're doing it at times, but exerting too much control when directing your child's play takes away from their ability to hone their own creative skills. It's like giving them a toy with instructions;

it signals that there's only one way to do things versus many. Also, over time, it creates a dependency on you to always provide ideas for play, which we can all agree is less than optimal for preserving your sanity, let alone preserving healthy skills for your child. So, let your child be the architect, both of their spaces (which we'll talk much more about in the next chapter) and of their play. Provide the materials, then get out of the way. That said, gentle encouragement and prompting is totally fine and may be helpful at first for kids who aren't used to tapping into their creativity.

Let go of perfection

The goal here is not a photoshoot-ready playroom or a home that looks as though children do not live there. Yes, keeping toys systematically organized and making sure there aren't too many of them looks nice, but this philosophy is not about aesthetics. In fact, it's not really about you at all (no offense). It's about what inspires your child. These spaces are meant to be functional *and* lived in. The bonus is that your child will know how and where to put everything away—and it's extremely reasonable to expect that they do—but the hope that things will be perfectly neat all the time is only setting you and your child up for frustration.

Let go of gatekeeping

We can be honest here: Most of the time, we parents (I'm looking at you especially, moms) are the ones getting the house organized and making sure everything has a place. But if you're keeping toys and other activity-related materials tucked away for any reason (especially for fear of a mess, which we'll get to in a minute), *you* become an obstacle to play. Over time, you become frustrated because everyone needs you to tell them where things are, and your child gets frustrated because they can't just help themselves. This is another reason why a dedicated play space stocked with age-appropriate activities is a huge win for all parties.

Hand over the keys

I once had to do an interview on television, so I enlisted the help of a stylist. She didn't ask me any questions about what kind of clothes I liked to wear or my favorite colors; she just assumed she knew best because she was the expert. And guess what? None of her selections spoke to me or felt like they reflected me in any way. But when I hired another stylist who immediately asked me about my preferences and involved me in the shopping process, I ended up with an outfit that I wear any chance I get.

As we go into more detail in the next chapter, you'll discover that one of the easiest ways to get your child excited about their new play spaces is to involve them in the planning and then let them drive, taking ownership of the process. Ask which activities they would like available, what materials they want on the art cart, which types of tools they would like in their play kitchen. On a common-sense level, this means they'll automatically have things that they're interested in doing. It also reinforces that you're listening, that you care, and that what they say matters, which helps build their self-esteem and can encourage self-expression. Additionally, it lets them know that they're in charge of their play and, by extension, in charge of their space. And with that comes a feeling of agency, responsibility, and pride. That's a pretty powerful and satisfying way to feel, when most of your day is spent being told what to do by adults!

One of the easiest ways to get your child excited about their new play spaces is to involve them in the planning.

The same thing applies to making sensory materials, whether it's playdough, glitter sensory bottles, ice paint, or other items and crafts. Involve your child. Don't just present these materials and expect them to go off and have a ball for an hour. I've found that it doesn't quite work that way. But when you make these things *with* your

child, they are going to feel invested in the process and are much more likely to engage with those materials for a longer period and in a more meaningful way.

Embrace the mess

Questions (and exclamations) I hear all the time include: "How do you just leave your art supplies out like that?!" and "Markers for your two-year-old?!" These kinds of statements are a direct reflection of the discomfort some parents feel around messier activities. And I understand the fear; our culture here in the States is very mess-phobic. But I always say, "You don't know until you try." As in, you don't know how your child will do unless you give them the opportunity to learn how to responsibly use an item, as well as the confidence that comes from experience.

I've heard from a lot of parents that when they give a child a tool with boundaries, such as scissors with the instruction "we only cut paper," or markers and "we only draw on paper," there's a much lower chance that this kid is going to go nuts, cutting their hair and drawing on the wall, than the kid who had to sneak to get access to those scissors or markers. Of course, if your child is going to be out of your sight, you also need to make sure any tools or materials you're giving them are going to be age appropriate.

You want to set up your child *and* yourself for success. Supply them with washable markers and paint, so if they do draw on the wall (or the table, their clothing, the dog), you'll be able to clean it up without too many issues—and without making them feel bad about it. If you do freak out (and I say this with love, because who hasn't been there at some point?), they're not going to want to take that creative risk again. As I like to point out to Marc, who is a major perfectionist: "What's the worst-case scenario?" We'll vacuum, sweep up, or wipe down the table. Or if that's not enough peace of mind—and it's not always the case for my husband, who has many strengths, but flexibility is not one of them—put down a wipeable surface before doing an art project, have your child get in the bath for that messier activity (we have a whole chapter about that!), or lay down a sheet or pop-up tub to collect sand or rice from a sensory box. Success is when your kid can do these things joyfully and independently, and you don't burn yourself out physically or mentally with the cleanup.

Be cool

Kids can smell their parents' desperation a million miles away. If you want them to hang out in their new play spaces, the last thing you want to do is hype them up or talk about them constantly. Set up the spaces, show your child where everything is, and let them be. The less pressure they feel, the more naturally they'll transition to this new setup.

When you show up, show up

Kids are much more willing to play by themselves if they know that their day will also be punctuated by intentional, present time with you. Call it the ten-minute miracle, call it feeding the meter, call it unplugging from the feed— whatever you want to call it, spending just ten minutes engaging in play with your kid (and without your phone) and being there with 100 percent of your attention is like parenting wizardry. Just that tiny amount of time communicates to your child that you're there for them in a significant way, which helps them feel seen, heard, and secure.[5]

Be patient and positive

While the twenty-one-days-to-a-new-habit formula has been busted as a myth, we now know that it can take as long as *eight months* for a new habit to form.[6] The same applies to independent play. You can't just snap your fingers and expect that your family's play culture will change. But don't get discouraged; the benefits far outweigh the small amount of initial time and effort it might take to get things up and running smoothly. And I promise that you'll eventually get there! If you follow the advice in this chapter and the next, continue to reevaluate your spaces and connect with your child over them, and come back to this book whenever you need to troubleshoot, you'll be in great shape. Plus, any step—even if it's teeny-tiny—is a win. If you simply declutter, it's a win. If you start thinking about how to offer your child more independence, it's a win. If you're just more mindful about the types of toys you bring into the house, it's a win. And it's certainly not all-or-nothing. I call this book a guide for a reason: This is a process. And I'm here for you every step of the way, cheering you on for your Mothercould moments.

Independent Play by Age

The length of time your child can realistically spend playing on their own will increase as they get older. Here's what's average, although you should follow the lead of your child and their needs:

- Newborn to six months: five to ten minutes
- Twelve months: fifteen minutes
- Eighteen months: fifteen to twenty minutes
- Two years: thirty minutes[7]

Start Them Young!

The more your child is exposed to independent play, the more comfortable with it they'll become. Even infants are perfect candidates for playing on their own. You could either try to juggle them and a pacifier in the carrier while you're prepping dinner, or you could let them have five to ten minutes of tummy time with a sensory mat. Or, if they're able to sit, set them next to a small selection of toys in a safe space where you can see them. (Including a play yard, if they're mobile.) No age is too young for safe, semi-monitored, independent play.

Common Independent Play Pitfalls

I can already hear your hesitation: *I tell my kids to go play all the time, and a minute later they're either destroying their playroom or complaining that they're bored. Or I give them art supplies, sensory games, or puzzles, and they just dump them out and walk away after thirty seconds.*

Valid. Real.

But if you're telling me that your child is *consistently* not engaged in their own activities, we need to dig a little bit deeper.

- Are the boundaries for play maybe a little too rigid? Is your child afraid to make a mess?

- Did they help set up their space or prepare the activity?

- Is their play space perfectly organized, to the point they perhaps got the message that it's not to be mussed?

- Are their toys difficult to reach or placed somewhere they're not able to access?

- Are there bins or boxes they are not able to open on their own?

- Is their play space too cluttered?

- Are toys tucked away in deep bins or in bins where they cannot see all the contents?

- Does their play space feature activities they are currently interested in?

- Are their toys too advanced? Not advanced enough?

- Are their toys too stimulating? Not engaging enough?

Each of these factors can affect how a child uses their space and how comfortable they feel there. Luckily, there are simple fixes for every single one. Some fixes are achieved through mindset shifts, others through decluttering and creative re-organizing. But all are found through the small steps I've outlined in this book, which yield very big results.

What About Electronics?

This might be a hot take, but I've never really been a fan of making things like television, tablets, and voice-activated technology such as Alexa a forbidden fruit. In my opinion, enforcing limitations or putting something on a pedestal only seems to make kids want those things more. Plus, it doesn't feel like it's preparing kids for real life, where they'll have access to pretty much all the technology they want. (Just ask any adult who can barely look away from their phone for a moment!) And, of course, I'd be naive not to acknowledge that for some families, these things need to stand in as a sitter. (Which goes for us, too, sometimes when we travel—though, as you'll read about in chapter 8, our girls tend to be more interested in their on-the-go play spaces.)

In our house, technology just gives us a few more tools for play. We set ourselves up for success by downloading age-appropriate apps and programs, and we have some boundaries in place—such as how early in the morning or late into the evening these things can be on—but other than that, our kids have a say in their technology diet. I've seen that after about twenty minutes of screen time, they're ready for the next thing.

If your child is used to leaning on TV and tablets for entertainment, don't assume they won't be willing to transition to other types of play. TV might be a big, fudgy piece of chocolate cake, but your new play spaces are like a delicious dessert buffet. You'll be amazed to see how just a few tantalizing new provisions (especially sensory materials like slime) or thoughtfully selected toys can pique the curiosity of the most devoted screen-timer. Or how effective it can be to incorporate screen time into their open-ended play, such as taking videos of their performances, "concerts," and science experiment outcomes, editing the footage, and watching it together as a family. They will still want that chocolate cake, and that's something we're all learning how to navigate as parents, but now they have other tasty offerings to fill their plates with too.

And if you are leaning on TV for entertainment, remember those mindset shifts we just talked about. If it's a control thing for you, because TV means your child isn't making a mess somewhere else in the house, create a space where they can find all the things they need for play without dumping out large containers, with the additional peace of mind that everything has a straightforward place to go when playtime is done. Any mess they make—and they *will* make a mess—can be contained and easy to handle.

The more I've dug into the research behind the benefits of sensory play, and the more I see those benefits unfolding in real time in my own home—not to mention in the thousands of homes of Mothercould community members—the more I'm convinced that it doesn't get much better than that. Here's why.

The Case for Sensory Play

As you may already know—or can tell by now—I'm a huge fan of sensory play. It helped me create a significant shift in how my daughter experienced the world, which in turn made me feel like the kind of mom who could do anything. Ever since, it's been the foundation of Mothercould and is still a staple of play in our house. While it's true that there are tons of store-bought options for kids' activities in their play spaces, for me, nothing will ever come close to a sensory project, which is why I've filled this book with some of my favorite recipes.

A big reason I think most families would benefit from these projects is that, generationally and culturally, we have moved a little too far from textures. Look at any baby registry: Most of those items are soft-on-soft-on-soft, not to mention the fact that like 90 percent of anything on there is dedicated to keeping things clean. Kids are encouraged to eat with utensils instead of their hands and to keep their meals tidy. When they grow up, they're not usually spending much of their free time outside, digging in the dirt and rolling down hills the way many of us did. So by the time they get to school, they're not really exposed to very many textures, even though it's those very textures and stimulations that help them develop on so many different levels. I often think that lack of exposure was at the root of Nicky's food aversions, which eventually went away after she acclimated to different sensations on her skin and on her plate.

It's inexpensive

Most sensory activities call for items you most likely have in your home (dish soap, flour, food coloring, water, rice), recycled items (toilet-paper and paper-towel rolls, paper, boxes, ice-pop sticks), or items you can buy for very little money.

It's durable

Many of these crafts can be used multiple times and kept for long periods of time when stored properly.

It's multipurpose

Sensory projects are the definition of *open-ended activities* and can be used many different ways. I love that they can grow with my kids too—the same sand tray that I made for my youngest, Ariana, to draw shapes with her finger is now what my six-year-old, Emma, uses as a fun way to practice writing sight words.

It's collaborative

Assembling these projects and materials is an opportunity for you to spend meaningful, focused time with your child and meet them where they are. But unlike playing with dolls or having them braid your hair, you're both working through the same process at the same time at the same level. They're also learning as you do so, whether it's simply listening to your language as you guide them through the process, counting, measuring, pouring, or stirring.

It's inclusive

There's no wrong way to engage in sensory play, and every child can reap the benefits.

It hones real-life fine-motor skills[8]

All my girls learned how to scoop and pour thanks to the often-repetitive motions of sensory play, which translated into them being able to pour juice and water at the dinner table and use utensils for their meals.

It supports cognitive development

Engaging the senses helps developing brains forge new neural connections,[9] which in time helps your child do more complex learning activities.

It strengthens problem-solving skills

Whether it's figuring out how to free toys from foam or icebergs, transporting water, or working with others to share materials, sensory activities model real-life scenarios and allow kids to practice these crucial skills.

It encourages language development

When children use the language centers of their brains while also using multiple senses, whether by narrating their experience to themselves or engaging with other children as they play, this stimulates both learning and language.[10]

It's calming

Stimulating the senses helps regulate the nervous system, which has a soothing effect on children.[11]

As for the assumption that sensory play is a mess or that it takes a lot of time, all I can say is, there are as many solutions as there are hang-ups. We do our projects in the kitchen, in the bathroom, or outside where they can be easily cleaned up, or we lay them out on a wipeable play mat, tray, or sheet. Each project typically takes about ten minutes to prep, which then leads to at least twenty minutes of independent play. That's thirty to forty-five minutes of connecting, learning, having fun, and feeling great as a parent—and I think that is well worth a few splatters or stray grains of rice.

Making the Dream a Reality

Everything we talked about in this chapter—all the promises, all the seemingly too-good-to-be-true visions—are yours for the taking. And not only that, but they're also not some far-off goal you can reach only if you quit your job or take out a small loan. I guarantee that if you follow the steps in the following chapters (even if they're baby ones), use the existing resources you already have (which is more than you think!), and put your kid in the driver's seat of their play, you're going to see a noticeable shift in your family dynamic.

But before we dig in, let's take a moment to remember what this is all about. Let go of the *shoulds* and all the pressure the world puts on you to get things right. Instead, let yourself feel gratitude for the opportunity to see the world through your child's eyes and to connect in a deep and meaningful way. You are about to bring more joy, more fun, more calm, more satisfaction, and more harmony into your home—and the path to get there is more play. Let's go!

Dreaming **Big**

Planning Your Spaces

A ll roads to successful play spaces start here. Want to create a room where your child will spend hours completely engrossed in activities of their own con- cocting? Follow the steps. Want a play outpost to keep little hands busy while you make dinner? Follow the steps. Want to keep your house from feeling packed to the brim with toys that your child only seems to ignore while begging for things to do? Follow the steps, follow the steps, follow the steps. And as your child gets older, or their interests change, or you need a refresher to troubleshoot or course correct, you can come back to these steps then too.

There's nothing particularly splashy or mind-blowing I'm recommending here, and no, there really aren't any hacks to getting around the initial work (*sorry!*), but remember that you can complete each step at your own pace and on your own terms. And I'm giving you all the resources and tips you'll need so it won't feel overwhelming. Think of this process as a kind of play in and of itself. It's one more opportunity for you to unearth new, exciting possibilities in your home, connect with your child in a meaningful way, and relieve at least some of the burdens that you've been lugging around as a parent who wants the best for their kids. Take a deep breath and dive in!

Step 1: Find Your Play "Hot Spots"

Before you start dreaming up how to create the ideal play spaces in your home, you first must figure out where these spaces are going to be and the function they'll need to serve. I have found that the optimal configuration is having *one primary play space* (or "home base") and then *several small spaces* (or "hot spots") throughout the house.

Even if you're lucky enough to have an enormous playroom, the reality is, your child is not going to want to play only in that room. So I suggest having one primary play space where a majority of the toys and activities will go, whether it is the *Playroom* (page 95) or the *Bedroom* (page 115), and a series of outposts.

When choosing where to put these outposts, think of them as strategically defining where you want your child to play (and, by extension, where you *don't* want them to play). If you have a younger child you'd like to keep an eye on while you're doing things around the house, go for the *Nook* or the *Mini* (page 125) in the same or adjacent spaces. If you tend to have early risers crashing your morning sleep-in, have a bedroom Magic Box (page 136) ready to go. To encourage safe outdoor play, set up the *Fresh-Air Play Space* (page 155). Before moving on to the next step, take a moment to flip through the chapters and sample spaces in part 2 (page 93) and create a plan for what and where your play spaces will be.

It Won't Feel like a Day Care!

I remember thinking, when we first had kids, that Marc and I weren't going to become those people whose home was completely overtaken by toys. I'd put so much effort into making our apartment—and later our house—look and feel beautiful, and I really didn't like the idea of it looking like a toy store had exploded inside of it. But I realized that if I was going to live my life peacefully while parenting three young girls, I would need to let toys be a part of the equation—even if they didn't necessarily match the decor.

When I applied the less-is-more philosophy I'd discovered when Nicky was little to my play "hot spots," I realized it didn't make my house feel like I was running a day care. In fact, I wasn't making *more* mess, I was *limiting* it. Because these supportive play spaces are small and limited to a select handful of toys, they fit seamlessly into your home (in a corner, under the TV console, in a basket on the shelf, under a desk, in a closet, in a cart, on a tray) and are easy to keep tidy—while also supercharging kids' desire to play. It's a major win-win.

Step 2: Take Everything Out

Not just the things you want to get rid of. Not just the few things you feel like moving. Not just the bins and boxes they're in. *Everything* comes out now! Even if you think you don't have that much stuff, I guarantee you have more than you think. As much work as I know this can be, and as messy as things might get before they get neat again, it's a crucial step in the process. By taking every last toy out of its current home, you are going to be able to see exactly what you have: the good, the bad, the tiny little bits and bobs that have been gathering dust for years. This will allow you to get rid of what you no longer need, as well as gain a sense of the space you have and the storage options you already own. Plus, you'll be starting with a completely clean slate—literally and figuratively: It's a great opportunity to wipe down all the nooks and crannies where these items had been stored.

I often see that people want to jump straight to organizing. They want to load up on all the cute little bins and baskets and then just chuck everything in there. But they've got it backward. Instead of running out to the store to bring *even more* things into the home and organizing a whole bunch of stuff they may not even need, I say let's first see what needs to go. Then, once it's cleaned out and sorted, you can see what you *maybe* need to go out and buy, which most likely will not be very much. In the long run, this will save you time and money, while also making your spaces clutter-free and much more functional.

For now, don't get too caught up with having a plan for every single item. Just focus on taking everything out and putting it all in one central area, such as your living room or kitchen.

Step 3: Declutter

Before you can move *anything* into your new play spaces, you've got to figure out what needs to be cleaned out of your toy stash. I don't care how on top of this you think you are; if you have kids, there are things to purge. For you, this will free up both physical space and mental space, while also allowing you to see exactly what you have. For kids, this will help them better appreciate the toys they actually love to play with.

Here are my general guidelines for giving your toy stash a much-needed reboot.

Anything broken or missing pieces is trash

Full stop. End of story. No one likes having to send things to a landfill, but that incomplete puzzle or that board game that's no longer fully functional because it's missing too many pieces is not doing anyone any favors. By embracing this new play-space philosophy, you'll not only be getting more mileage out of your existing toys, but you'll also be more tuned in to what kinds of toys and activities your child will get the most use out of. And that means sending less to the trash in the future. The *only*

exceptions to this rule are repurposing and recycling, but I urge you to strongly consider how many of these items you realistically need.

Another way to get just a little more mileage out of these items is to repurpose some of the components. More on this just below.

One kid's trash is another kid's treasure

The saying is true; any toys our kids have outgrown or no longer play with are going to kids who will appreciate them so much more. Churches and synagogues are excellent places to donate toys to, and they typically have built-in programs for donating these items. You could also ask local day cares if they need toys, or take them to a secondhand shop.

Repurpose it for the Magic Box

You have my permission to save some tchotchkes, trinkets, figurines, and other small stray toys for this small (*small!*) stash. You'll read more about this on page 136. It's a great in-case-of-emergency distraction you can pull out anytime, and you won't need to purchase anything, because chances are you already have all the odds and ends you'll ever need. It's also like a little time capsule, because kids tend to be excited to revisit these things that otherwise get lost in the shuffle.

Recycle it for sensory play

Similar to the Magic Box, you can use board game pieces, large wooden puzzle pieces, or even the wells on those large wooden puzzles as accessories for sensory play. Fill those wells with dyed rice, use the large pieces as part of a tracing activity, bury the stray game pieces in kinetic sand—get creative! That said, this is *not* me telling you to keep every last item. Give yourself a limit of one pouch or small bin to fill, and the rest *goes*.

Allow for some second chances

When a playroom has been completely packed with toys, you might wonder, *Did she not play with this toy because she didn't want to or because she didn't have access to it?* With some toys, you won't be sure whether your child is still into them. You're welcome to see if these things receive more attention once everything is cleaned out. Or maybe the toys go away for a few months and then get reintroduced in the toy rotation to see if they get played with. But if they still don't make the cut in their new home, it's time to go.

Allow for some sentimentality

Whenever Marc and I are cleaning out our toy stash, we always make sure to do it together, because if it were up to me, I'd keep just about everything—just for the sentimental memories. Marc, on the other hand? Ruthless. Just joking—he's not completely coldhearted. But he recognizes there's a happy medium, and he's right.

Some toys that your child has grown out of might be okay to hang on to. Whether you're stashing them away for future children (we have the sweetest videos of all three of our girls playing with some of the same toys) or even grandchildren, you have my permission to hold on to these items. But that does not mean you need to keep bins and bins and bins full. Be realistic about the toys that will go the distance and how much storage space you're willing to sacrifice. I assure you, there will always be more toys where those came from.

So if you're also someone who has difficulty letting go of things, it can be helpful to work with a partner—your spouse, a friend, a family member—who can provide a counterbalance and objectivity.

Let go of the guilt

Remember that you're not getting rid of the one toy car they love; you're getting rid of the ten they don't. This also applies to letting go of things that were gifts, especially from someone who means a lot to you. If your child hasn't played with an item in months and still doesn't seem interested after it gets a fresh new home, it's time to pass it on to someone else who may really enjoy it. And for those toys you saved up to buy and give to your child as an extra-special extravagance, think about it this way: You've now given *two* gifts—one to your child and one to the next child who gets to love and appreciate it.

Keep it open-ended

Your child will get so much more mileage out of toys that have more than one function during play. Scarves become tablecloths for dolls to dine on, or blankets to tuck them in for nap time, or capes for a superhero rescue. Blocks can be for building towers and matching colors with other items in the room. While it's okay for some of your toy selection to be single purpose—think remote-control cars, battery-operated "speaking" toys, branded play sets—consider making them a smaller portion of your inventory.

Make toy-buying resolutions

Use this experience to inform your toy buying in the future. When purchasing something new, ask yourself: *Is it open-ended? Will it get used? Is it environmentally friendly?* Also, consider spending a little more on toys that have longevity or may be heirloom worthy, such as wooden puzzles versus paper, or high-quality dolls whose parts tend to stay intact. These are the types of toys that can be handed down to younger siblings before being donated and going on to have an even longer life, which is an investment both in your family and in the community.

Decide how to involve your child

While I do think involving your child in the play-space-planning process is a great thing, I strongly recommend having them sit this step out. You'll be able to get rid of the things that need to be purged without encountering any big feelings. And for most kids, when something is out of sight, it's out of mind. Plus, as I said before, you won't be getting rid of anything that has any significance to your child.

If you have older kids who aren't too attached to every single toy, you could do a first pass of gathering all the low-hanging fruit and then allowing them to choose which items to part with. Or you can simply show them what you've collected to be given away and allow them to say goodbye. It's a great empathy- and life-skill-building opportunity to teach them about letting go and sharing something they once loved with someone else.

Alternatively, if you're concerned about whether your child is ready to handle that, take care of the gathering and cleaning-out without them, then let them choose which toys will go directly into the play spaces and which will go into storage for the next play rotation.

Repeat

This is not a one-and-done process. As long as you have kids living in the house, there will be toys to declutter. Every household is different in terms of how frequently you need to take inventory, but I recommend doing a full clean-out once or twice a year. If you've set up your play spaces using the guidelines in this chapter, you'll know the exact moment when things no longer have a comfortable place in the system. But it will take a fraction of the time the first one did. I can promise you that.

Step 4: Organize by Type

This is when the magic starts to happen, because organized materials and toys are not only more appealing to play with, they're also easier to put away *and* look great too. (Is there *anything* more satisfying than everything having a place? No. No, there's not.)

To organize by type, you'll need to take all the items left after decluttering and sort them. Before moving anything around, grab a pad of paper (I like sticky notes) and a pen and make labels for each of the major categories: dolls, cars, kitchen, dress-up, blocks, art, puzzles. It's okay to leave things general for now.

Give each category some physical space with plenty of room to spread out, then begin placing all your up-to-date toys in those categories. As you do, look for natural subsets within them, such as:

- Kitchen: utensils, plates, food, appliances, aprons, oven mitts
- Dolls: clothing, accessories, furniture, dolls
- Dress-up: clothing, gloves, masks, jewelry, crowns, wigs
- Cars: track pieces and cars
- Art: paintbrushes, paint, pens, markers, crayons, scissors

Step 5: Meet Your Players

This is a fun one. Think about who is playing with these toys and play spaces and what their interests are. This will help you figure out which of your existing toys to keep, as well as which toys might be ready to go and what new materials you might want to invest in. It will also guide your organization in the following step, when you begin to plan your play spaces. For example, if you have a baby or toddler, you'll want the toys to be at their level so they're enticing and reachable. If you have a mix of older and younger children, you can arrange things vertically so little ones can't get into activities that may not be age appropriate, such as toys with smaller pieces. Don't get caught up with what this might look like down the road when they're older; plan for your child right at this moment.

To help get the creativity flowing for you and your child, here are some play categories to begin thinking about.

- ▶ Dress-up and pretend play: Think superheroes, doctor/veterinarian, princesses, and firefighters—anything involving a costume and accessories

- ▶ Sports and gross-motor skills: anything involving climbing, throwing, bouncing, swinging, jumping, tumbling, biking, and scootering

- ▶ Cars and trucks

- ▶ Music and instruments

- ▶ Technology and gaming

- ▶ Arts and crafts and DIY

- ▶ Literacy: books plus reading- and writing-related activities

- ▶ Numeracy: math- and counting-related activities

- ▶ Sensory activities and science experiments

- ▶ Dolls and stuffies

- ▶ Puzzles and games

- ▶ Building: blocks, magnetic tiles, and LEGO bricks

- ▶ Kitchen and cooking

- ▶ Play "sprinkles": multiuse materials that enhance play—scarves, glitter sensory bottles, flashlights, and traffic cones

Step 6: Plan Your Space

At this point in the process, you'll know what types of toys are going to go into your play space or spaces. And you'll know that a large portion of them will be put away in storage for eventual toy rotations. You'll also know about how much room you have for toy display, at least at a glance. This can also depend on which type or types of play-space arrangement you've chosen from Part 2 (page 93). So now it's time to figure out how exactly to do that. Start by asking yourself these two questions about each space.

1. **Do I have the infrastructure to *display* these items (such as furniture)?**
   For example:
   Do I have a shelf for puzzles and/or books?
   Do I have low cubbies for my toddler's toys?
   Do I have wall hooks for hanging dress-up clothing?
   Do I have a table to accommodate art or sensory projects?
   Can I maximize the storage I have by adding a vertical element for my older children?

2. **Do I have the storage systems I need to *contain* these items?**
   For example:
   Do I have shallow bins for doll accessories?
   Do I have a small basket for board books?
   Do I have a caddy for drawing materials?

As for what exactly these storage and furniture items might be, I encourage you to check out "Chapter 10: Storage Solutions," on page 203, where I've included my favorite organizational items and how to use them. But before you go rushing out to buy anything, consider a few things first.

You may already have these items

Check your existing play spaces or other rooms. When it comes to setting up hot spots in shared spaces, such as the living room or your bedroom, some items might be able to do double duty.

You may be able to freshen up some things

Don't be quick to toss existing shelving or other furniture that's seen its share of action. Even if you weren't planning to get rid of these items, consider giving them a makeover anyway! Your space will be more inviting because of it.

▶ **To remove stickers:** Run a hair dryer over the sticker for about fifteen seconds to loosen the adhesive, then gently peel off the sticker. Give the surface a wipe with a wet cloth, and done! You could also use a putty knife for this, but most of the time you won't need it.

▶ **To remove marker:** You just need a cleanser and cloth. If permanent marker has entered the mix, spray the marks with sport spray sunscreen and allow it to sit for five to ten seconds. Wipe it off with a clean cloth.

▶ **To remove crayon:** Window cleaner is extremely effective at dissolving crayon marks. Spray, wipe, done.

▶ **To disinfect:** Add white vinegar to a spray bottle and give everything a spritz. If you're sensitive to the vinegar smell—which does dissipate just a few seconds after spritzing—you could dilute the vinegar with water, with a ratio of 1:1.

You might find storage items secondhand

Whether it's furniture, organizers, or items to help round out the toys you have (such as an upgraded play kitchen, additional racetrack pieces, or LEGO bricks), you're likely to find what you need from a local parenting group online or your local secondhand shop. You'll not only be getting those items at a fraction of the price of buying them new, but you're also saving them from a landfill.

Next, depending on how large the play space is that you're planning, you might find it helpful to draw the space (no judgment here; it doesn't need to be architect level or to scale) and plug in the furniture pieces or other large items that you'd like to include, if applicable. You can then add little notes about where certain types of toys would work best.

Labeling

Whether you label your storage containers is up to you. Do I think it looks nice? Yes. Can it be beneficial? Absolutely. But it isn't necessary, and it should definitely not be the thing to keep you from organizing your play spaces. If you've followed the steps in chapter 2 and use an organizing system that allows your child to see everything in plain sight, they won't need to rely on labels to know where things go.

If you do want to label your shelves and bins, you have options. You could purchase a label maker, or you could use painter's tape or plain labels and a permanent marker. If your child isn't yet reading, print symbols or pictures of the items.

I also highly recommend that you label your items when they go out of the play rotation and into storage, especially if you're transferring them into pouches or containers you cannot see through.

Step 7: Add Things Back In

This is where our blueprints from step 6, question 2 will come in handy. They will give you more specific guidance for how to set up a space, depending on its location, size, and function. And this is when you'll put your sales cap on and think like a toy-store merchandiser. Your most popular items—maybe your magnetic tiles or your playdough—go front and center. Then next to them could be things that haven't been huge hits in the past, but they might be more interesting if they're laid out next to the main attractions. (And if not, these will get phased out and donated.) Everything should have plenty of space around it, just like on a store shelf. Don't be afraid of white space; just because you have twelve shelves does not mean you need to fill twelve shelves. The most crucial element: Everything should be *visible*. If it's out of sight, it's out of mind.

The other benefit of not packing your shelves full of toys, especially in multiuse spaces in your home, is that it makes it easy to move everything when you have company. And don't forget, you won't need to find a place for every single toy, because you'll be putting things away for your toy rotation.

The Ideal Play Space . . .

Is a dedicated space

Nothing else happens there but play. Even if it's a corner of a bedroom, a nook in the living room, or a cart in the kitchen, these spaces are more effective and easier to maintain if they are devoted entirely to play. Meaning, when your kid enters that space, they're instantly inspired by their materials for play, they're not distracted by anything they're not supposed to be playing with, and they know they can have as much fun as they want in that space without repercussions. This also makes these spaces easier to keep clean and organized, because nothing other than toys comes in or out of it.

Is readily accessible to the child

There's nothing they can't reach, nothing they can't open without assistance, and nothing they can't participate in without supervision.

Is safe

All materials have been vetted for any potential hazards, and all furniture is safely secured to the wall. If your space accommodates children ranging in age and the older children have access to activities with smaller pieces that may be a choking hazard, be sure they know that little ones are not to have access to those items. If you can't trust that that won't happen, that activity is not appropriate for that space. Store it for a future day when it is.

Follows the Costco model

This store limits your options within a category, removing indecision, overwhelm, and perceived dissatisfaction from the consumer. That's why you don't see seventeen kinds of toothbrushes and six kinds of peanut butter at Costco. In a play space, that means offering only one or two activities in each play category, and offering a variety of categories. Maybe it's alternating between princess dress-up and doctor dress-up, magnetic tiles and wooden blocks, and watercolors and finger paints.

Caters to the children who will use it

If you have more than one child and expect all your kids to want to play in your playroom, that room needs to reflect each of their interests and needs. Storing things vertically is the perfect solution, because you can put activities for older children up top where only they can reach them. On the other hand, mini hot spots meant to occupy little ones while you're getting things done don't necessarily have to appeal to older kids.

Has things your child is interested in

This might feel like a big, fat *duh*, but don't forget to let your child be the architect of their space. Ask them what activities they're excited about and follow their interests, then build the space around their existing toys as well as new activities they want access to.

Has skill-building activities

Think about what age-appropriate skills your child is actively working on. It's a great way to enhance your play space's activities. This doesn't mean giving them homework or being overbearing, but offering play opportunities that reinforce those skills. Think counting, reading, writing, color and shape identifying, and other skills that can be learned through play.

Is consistent with your home

These days there are so many aesthetically pleasing yet inexpensive storage options that can be coordinated with your home's palette and style. Don't settle for an eyesore.

Step 8: Set Up a Toy Rotation System

This is the secret sauce for a successful play space. By putting out only a small portion of your toys and activities, you're removing friction between decision and play while also fending off clutter. And at the same time, you'll have a back stock of toys that will keep things feeling exciting and fresh for a long time.

Implementing a rotation system isn't complicated. After curating a selection of toys with some variety and plenty of white space, you'll store the rest. Then, every few weeks (more or less, depending on you, your time, and your child), you'll swap out some displayed toys for stored ones. These will feel new, even if they have been in your house for years. Once you sense your child is losing interest in the current selection, that's a good indication that it's time for another rotation.

Here are a few more helpful guidelines:

Establish an accessible storage system for out-of-rotation toys

I like bundling loose pieces of an activity or play set into reusable zip-top bags, labeling each bag, and stacking them in bins or large tubs. (Empty suitcases can also do the trick.) If closet space is limited, consider under-bed storage, garage storage, cabinet storage, or storage at the very top of your children's bedroom closets.

Don't rotate the foundational toys that get played with the most
> This usually includes those core open-ended toys that can get folded into almost any kind of play, such as scarves, balls, and building blocks.

Store a large portion of toys
> This also applies to holidays, birthdays, and any other time there's a big influx of new toys. It's not a punishment, and it's not something you need to make a big deal out of with your child, but subtly nudge a selection of those toys into storage. It will make the new items your child plays with immediately feel even more special, and then they'll get a second or third boost of excitement when the remaining toys enter the rotation.

Consider rotating the stations in the play space as well
> This creates an even bigger wow factor while also offering your child a fresh perspective, which can spark new and interesting play. Moving the blocks next to the dolls might inspire castle building, while flashlights next to the sensory glitter bottles could prompt a large-scale art installation, and shifting the reading nook to another corner might create an even more enticing spot to curl up in.

Bring in the holidays

Timing a rotation with a holiday could bring an infusion of themed books, toys, and decorations.

Step 9: Maintenance and Cleaning Up

This piece is crucial for the success of your play space. Luckily, if you've thoughtfully completed the preceding steps, your new space is much more likely to be effortlessly maintained. When everything has a home, there's a place to put everything away. And when your child knows where they can find each toy, they also know where they can put each one back. But because we're talking about kids here, cleaning up may not be so straightforward.

What ultimately keeps a system working is when everybody collectively understands it and takes ownership of it. If only the adults—or one adult—oversee the maintenance, then the whole system falls apart. Instead, make it clear to your child that this is their territory. And with that independence and freedom comes, yes, responsibility—another great life lesson for them. The maintenance, of course, needs to be age appropriate for your child, but it's not too crazy an idea to expect that even toddlers can be aware of where their toys go: Food goes in the play kitchen; books go in the basket; stuffies go on the shelf. It really can—and should—be as simple as that.

As much as possible, we like to encourage our kids to clean up as they go—meaning, they'd ideally put away one activity before moving on to the next. But because we are encouraging them to play independently, and because we would be defeating the whole purpose of that independent play if we stood

around helicopter-parenting them, sometimes their play spaces are left less than tidy. Just remember that gentle reminders to clean up go a long way, and if your child is younger than eight or nine, they may need you to be a little more hands-on with the cleaning up. And no, that's not defeating the purpose of independent play; think of all that uninterrupted time you got back to yourself!

That said, you've already set them up for success with how straightforward cleanup will be, thanks to your new systems. Over time, and with consistency, cleaning up becomes second nature for your child—like brushing their teeth before bed. It's just something you do to take care of something that's important to you. You can also sweeten the deal by making it fun; turn it into a game or a race, or do what we do and play your kids' favorite music to make it feel like less of a chore. The girls sing and dance their way through cleaning, which helps the time pass more quickly.

The most important thing to keep in mind is that your house isn't going to look magazine-shoot-ready all the time—and that's okay! We want our kids to learn the valuable skill of independence, not perfection. As I like to say: There's a big difference between "messy" and "lived in."

The Steps at a Glance

Step 1: Find Your Play "Hot Spots"
Consult part 2 on page 93 to choose which play spaces you'd like to set up.

Step 2: Take Everything Out
Every last toy, trinket, and knickknack.

Step 3: Declutter
Identify which items will be donated and which can be thrown away.

Step 4: Organize by Type
Sort the remaining toys by category.

Step 5: Meet Your Players
Give some thought to who will be using the play spaces, their interests, and their needs.

Step 6: Plan Your Space
Consider what will be going in and how it will be organized and displayed.

Step 7: Add Things Back In
Select which toys will be on offer in each space.

Step 8: Set Up a Toy Rotation System
Create a storage plan for toys not currently being offered and monitor for when kids might be ready for a fresh infusion.

Step 9: Maintenance and Cleaning Up
If you took it out, put it back, preferably where it came from.

Troubleshooting

If there ever comes a point when things are not going as smoothly as you'd hoped—your child is resisting playing independently, your child is still asking for help all the time, or your play spaces have devolved into complete chaos—it's time to go back to the basics. Ask yourself a few questions.

- Did my kids help shape the space?
- Are the activities I've provided them with age appropriate and engaging?
- Is there too much to choose from?
- Are the storage containers easy enough to access without assistance?
- Are my expectations too high in terms of how long my child can be expected to play on their own or how they'll interact with the space?
- Have I clearly communicated my expectations and boundaries?
- Have I given this new system enough time to become second nature? (This will vary from family to family, based on the ages of your children and their personalities. Give it time!)

You Don't Need a Bigger House

We all know the feeling. You've got everything sorted into categories, and everything has a home; you might even have a storage plan and toy rotation all worked out. And then, like some terrible toy witchcraft, you somehow run out of room. Suddenly, you can barely cram one more book on the bookshelf or toy car in the bin. The first thought likely to come to mind is, *This wouldn't happen if we had more space.* Followed quickly by, *And this system just doesn't work for us.*

The good news is that you're wrong. On both counts.

First, you could have three jumbo-sized playrooms, and you would still feel like you had nowhere to put things—because that's how toys (like most of the things we buy) work. If left relatively unchecked, they will slowly and steadily trickle into our lives . . . and then never, ever leave.

Second, the issue here is not with the system; it's with the stuff. When all your bins and baskets and cubbies are full to bursting, the solution is not to buy more bins and baskets and cubbies. It's to figure out what could reasonably go. I get that that's not exactly the easiest route. But my guess is that if you asked yourself the tough question—*Do my kids truly still love playing with this item?*—you will be able to let some things go.

Remember: The goal is to provide your child with the raw materials for play, and then let their imagination do the rest. You can do it, they can do it, and *everyone* will be happier for it.

Recipe

Upcycled Crayons

Instead of tossing those broken crayons, you can easily transform them into like-new ones in fun new shapes.

What You'll Need

Crayons, broken into pieces

Instructions

1. Soak the crayons in warm water just long enough to loosen the labels. Peel off the labels and discard.

2. Arrange the crayon pieces in the wells of an oven-safe silicone mold. Break or chop them to fit if you need to. The mold can have whatever shapes you like or happen to have on hand. Place the mold on a small sheet pan.

3. Transfer the tray and mold to the oven and heat at 275°F until the crayons fully melt.

4. Allow the new crayons to cool completely in the mold before popping out the upcycled crayons and adding them to your arts and crafts rotation.

The **Play Spaces**

PART 2

CHAPTER 3

The **Playroom**

The playroom, or an entire room dedicated to play, is the ultimate home base. It's more like a play *world*, built for complete ownership by your child and devoted to the things they love to do. For them, it's a special escape, a place that's separate from the rest of the house, which tends to be your domain and is associated with more grown-up or boring day-to-day things—the *dining* room, the *bed*room, the *bath*room. But the *play*room? That's a place where kids can be kids and imaginations can run free, which has benefits way beyond just playing. And while your child wants to be in there for hours, making up new games or challenging themselves to build the coolest racetrack, you get the peace of mind that they're in a safe place, strengthening new skills, learning about ownership and responsibility, forming connections, and making memories.

If you are lucky enough to have this kind of real estate in your home—which we acknowledge is a luxury and is not required to facilitate independent play—this is where a majority of play will happen, and it should be set up accordingly. It is *not*, however, a place to simply stuff all the toys.

If you do not have a room that can become a dedicated play space, again, this is not a deal-breaker. Skip ahead to chapter 4 for more information about bedroom-based play spaces (page 115) or to chapter 5 for the nook (page 125), both of which can be very effective play headquarters in a home.

Optimizing Your Space

The playroom differs from other play areas because there's a lot more space to fill. While the steps in chapter 2 will set you up for success, I recommend drawing a blueprint so you can divide the room into *play zones*.

First, make a rough outline of your space. (Drawing a square or rectangle on a piece of paper is perfectly fine!) Next, divide the room into quadrants, or quarters. Then assign each quadrant a general category of play. Maybe it's building, imaginative play (dress-up, play kitchen), reading, and arts and crafts. Or video games, building, gross-motor play or sports, and science experiments. So when you put things back, you know that all the accessories and materials associated with that quadrant will be right there in plain sight—not across the room, not tucked away somewhere, but right there in the correct zone.

Creating a blueprint with play zones will also help you know a few things:

- how much room you have

- where to put your toys and how to group them

- what kind of storage you need

- how to shift things when it comes to the next toy rotation

- how to inspire different variations of play (for example, introducing new materials for experiments or arts and crafts, or adding doctors' instruments and clothing to the imaginative play area)

And it helps children know the following:

- what kind of play materials are on the play "menu"

- where exactly their toys are (for example, the play food is directly next to the play kitchen, not in the third bin from the left in the downstairs closet)

- where exactly to put their toys away

Another approach to these play zones, for those with more than one kid, is to divide them up by your children, especially if they have very different interests. Age isn't so much a factor, since the older children's toys, which aren't yet age appropriate for the little ones, should be stored up higher and out of reach of little hands. No matter how you organize these zones, the payoffs remain the same!

Make It a Place They Want to Be In

Creating an inspiring playroom doesn't have to require hiring a decorator or shelling out a ton of money on aesthetic elements. I mean, let's be honest: All your child's favorite toys are in there—it's not like they need much more incentive to get in there and play! That said, kids want to feel good in their own spaces as much as we do in ours. So I highly recommend taking some time to put a little thought into how to make your playroom the kind of place you'd want to be in. Here are some general rules of thumb for kid-friendly spaces, none of which call for huge investments of time or money.

Stick with light, bright colors

They're more inviting, not unlike your favorite toy store! If you paint the walls, opt for a high-gloss or eggshell finish (never matte) because they're wipeable. You can also introduce color through artwork, including framed pieces your child has created, area rugs, cushions, and wipeable play mats.

Ensure good lighting

This is especially key if your space doesn't have a window.

Hang mirrors

Mirrors not only help reflect the light to make a space feel inviting, but they also help small spaces look larger. They're also super functional if your play space has a dress-up area. Just be sure to choose mirrors that are shatterproof and securely attach them to the wall.

Make it comfortable

Add something soft underfoot that can double as comfortable floor seating, such as an area rug or wipeable play mat, or consider investing in cozy places for snuggling up with a book, such as a child-sized sofa or beanbag chairs.

Do I Need an Arts and Crafts Table?

The short answer is, nope! A playroom—or any room—can most certainly be a playroom without a table that was specifically created for this purpose. The most important thing is that you have a table somewhere in your home that has the clear designation of "this is where we paint, draw, and do art." This will help avoid any unwanted messes in other places. Add an art caddy or lazy Susan on top, or place an art cart nearby, and they're good to go.

My kids love sitting at the kitchen table, but I will say that one of the best (very inexpensive) investments we made was a child-sized round table for their playroom. They can sit with their feet firmly on the floor (an occupational therapist's tip to encourage better posture), and because it's round, it's easy to add more chairs as needed when other kids come over to play.

Setting Up Your Child for Success with Art Supplies

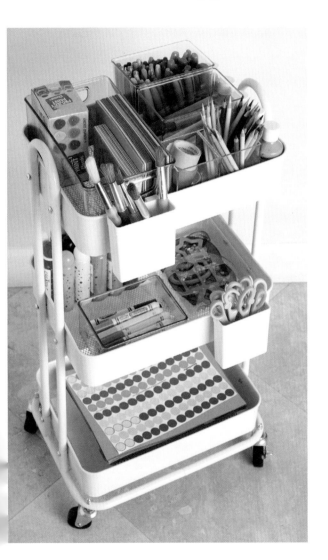

What three playthings could be in a parenting haunted house? Unattended scissors, paint, and markers. But my experience with these tools is that they're just like anything else you want your child to respect and use responsibly. And because we treat these items with respect, my kids don't need me to micromanage their arts and crafts play. Here's how to build healthy boundaries around arts and crafts materials that set up your child for independent play while also building trust and confidence.

- ▶ Start by setting up your arts and crafts table, cart, or tray.

- ▶ Bring your child to the space and show them the materials there. If they're older, give them a gentle reminder that these items are meant to be used on paper and only paper. (Not a dissertation, not a commandment, just a gentle reminder.)

- ▶ If they're younger, show them in a hands-on way how to use these tools. Take their hand in yours and demonstrate how to use the scissors or draw with marker while talking about how these things are for paper only.

- ▶ You know your child best. If you think you're setting them up for failure because they have difficulty following directions or struggle with impulse control, start small with low-stakes materials such as crayons and colored pencils. The older they get, the more responsibility they can have.

For the Gamer

Yes, video games are another type of play. I respect that every family has its own boundaries when it comes to kids' use of electronics, but for us, we've always found that the less "forbidden" we make age-appropriate shows and video games, the less hyperfocused our kids are on them. If your child loves video games, consider making that a part of the playroom versus a separate activity. This way, they'll also be surrounded by many other activity options—ideally many that they've shown an interest in—which may help reduce how much they're leaning on video games for entertainment.

If part of your challenge is easing up how much time your child spends playing video games, consider coming from a positive, additive place versus a negative, limiting place. That means, instead of trying to take this type of play away, see if you can challenge them to incorporate play into their video gaming. Maybe it's drawing pictures of the characters or re-creating some of the challenges, such as constructing racetracks or even acting them out in real life. Remember, independent play is a muscle that needs to be strengthened, and some kids need a little bit more practice. Meet your child where they are, continue to give them great ingredients for play, and, over time, you both will find a balance that feels good for everyone.

> **Independent play is a muscle that needs to be strengthened.**

Recipe

Sensory Glitter Bottles

I love the idea of a project that becomes a toy, especially one that provides so many possibilities for play. Sensory glitter bottles are very high on my list of recommended crafts because they're made with things you most likely already have, and they can grow with your child. Babies can stare at these forever because they're like mesmerizing little lava lamps. Plus, the slow-moving materials interacting with one another helps the brain with mood regulation, which makes these super calming.[12] As your child gets older, they can use glitter bottles for fairy play, color sorting, or shining a flashlight through to make a rainbow on the wall. Plus, they're pretty enough to be their own decoration.

What You'll Need

Plastic bottle (Any size or shape; you could use a recycled bottle or purchase one. A 13.6-ounce juice bottle works nicely and is a little sturdier.)

Clear glue (Hair gel, corn syrup, or glitter glue will also work.)

Fine glitter and/or metallic confetti

Food coloring

Hot water

Hot-glue gun (Superglue will also work.)

Recipe continued on next page.

Instructions

1. Fill the bottle ⅓ of the way with the glue. Add your glitter and/or confetti, 1 to 2 drops of the food coloring, and enough hot water to fill the bottle.

2. Tightly seal the bottle and shake well. Adjust the color with more food coloring, if desired, or add more glitter if needed. Use the hot-glue gun to glue the cap in place. This is an important step for avoiding leaks or accidents.

Have Some Fun

▶ Make a fall-themed bottle with confetti leaves and orange and yellow glitter.

▶ Make ocean-themed bottles with blue water, fish, and play seaweed.

▶ Make flower-themed bottles with flower-shaped confetti and matching shades of water and/or glitter.

▶ Make space-themed bottles with dark-blue water and glitter, plus planet-shaped confetti. (Bonus if the planets glow in the dark!)

Portable Play Ideas

THE CART

A tiered cart on wheels is the ideal play-space system. It's inexpensive, it can hold all the things you need for a particular kind of play, it has a small footprint, and it's mobile. There's no end to how you can deck out a cart to outfit your child's play, and you can tuck any number of carts throughout your house, whether next to a table in a playroom or nook, or as its own traveling mini play space. It really is the best bang for your buck.

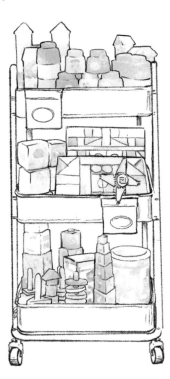

Depending on what you fill your cart with, you may want to think about organizers or smaller bins and caddies that fit inside the tiers, so you're not just tossing all your crayons and markers in there and calling it a day. As with anything else in your play spaces, you want these play materials to be visible and categorized, so they're easy to grab and easy to stash. Some of these carts come preloaded with organizers or caddies, which makes this even more of a no-brainer!

You can work a cart into your play spaces in so many ways.

The Art Cart: Load it up with their favorite art supplies and paper. Done and done.

The LEGO Cart: Add containers for sorting the bricks by size, shape, or color, and then leave space for works in progress and finished masterpieces.

The Magnetic Tile Cart: Similar to the LEGO cart, you can sort the tiles by color, shape, or size and leave room for your child's creations.

The Reading Cart: Make a mobile library by stacking their books on each tier. If you have multiple children, they can each have their own tier.

The Sensory Cart: Stock the cart with all the components for sensory activities, such as dyed rice, playdough, slime, or kinetic sand, plus any trinkets and tools.

CHAPTER 4

The Bedroom Play Space

Your child's bedroom is their home within your home. It's their sanctuary, somewhere to be alone or have privacy. And it's also somewhere where they can have a little more control over their surroundings and their space, which is what makes it so perfect as a place to play.

If you do not have a playroom as a primary play space, your child's bedroom—or their side of their bedroom, if they share with a sibling—is the next best thing. It's a great way to keep kids' things in kids' spaces, while still giving them a special place that feels like it belongs to them. One caveat: It's not the place to be setting up sensory or otherwise messy play; leave that for the kitchen or the bathroom.

If you do have a playroom, the bedroom can be a nice additional play-space option, especially if your child likes having a little cocoon where they can dig into their creativity and independence. But you don't need two primary play spaces; that's when you get into too-many-toys, not-enough-time territory.

Optimizing Your Space

Exactly how much storage you need in this space is going to depend on whether it's their primary play space. If it's not, decide how many toys are appropriate, given your child's preferences and your family's culture. For example, would you rather your child gravitate toward their room or more toward communal areas for their play? The don't-touch-my-stuff child is a great candidate for a bedroom hangout, whereas the FOMO (Fear of Missing Out) child who always wants to be around the family may simply need some books in there.

When setting up your bedroom play space, keep this important rule in mind: *Playthings and life things should be stored separately*. Ideally, clothing, shoes, and accessories would not share a home with your child's toys. This is for a few reasons.

1. It creates a mental separation between the fun things and the not-so-fun things. You want your child to be inspired to play near their toys—and only their toys.

2. It smooths the transition from playing to the other important things your child does in their room, such as sleeping or homework.

3. It's easier to keep things neat and organized, because everything has a home. And trust me, you do not want your child's entire closet to become fair game for play.

Here's how to get the most out of your bedroom playroom.

Use dressers

for housing everyday items like clothing and accessories, so you can dedicate the closet to a play area.

Think vertically

Bedrooms tend to be smaller spaces, so shelves that take advantage of height—especially for older kids— are a good idea.

Tiered rolling carts

(see page 112) can be tucked into narrow spaces when play is over.

Over-the-door storage

maximizes otherwise unused space. You can store figurines or dolls in a shoe organizer, or use a sweater organizer as a cubby system for individual toys or arts and crafts materials.

Built-in storage

doesn't necessarily mean shelling out for custom carpentry. There are plenty of inexpensive options, such as freestanding closets.

Wall-mounted book racks

help keep a selection of books visible (versus bookshelves, where books tend to get crammed in and disappear), while also keeping valuable floor space free.

Decorative displays

These could be themed shelves for showcasing your child's favorite cars, dolls, LEGO creations, or any other collections they might have. These double as both storage and decoration.

Other Considerations:

- ▶ **Add a desk** for an extra play surface.

- ▶ **Use floor baskets** along the wall for a baby or toddler, but put only one or two toys in each. Board books also work well "shelved" in these.

- ▶ **Hang a bulletin board** for displaying art.

- ▶ **Lay down a rug** if you have hardwood floors, ideally one that's washable. (I love the rugs that have a machine-washable top layer.)

- ▶ **Under-bed storage and upper-closet storage** can be useful for out-of-rotation toys.

A Gentle Reminder

While a bedroom serves many purposes, it's ultimately for rest and sleep. If your child also uses the space as a playroom, be sure to adjust your routine accordingly. Maybe before dinner they put their toys away, so afterward, when they're getting ready for bed, their room is a calmer environment. This also teaches them an important life skill: No one enjoys sleeping in a messy room. If your child likes a little playtime before bed (and who doesn't?), be sure the toys in that space aren't too stimulating.

Corner

Bedroom setup . . .

Nook

Bunks

The **Nook** and the **Mini**

CHAPTER 5

T he *nook* and the *mini* are your play-space hot spots. They're like little docking stations for your child to hang out in, especially when you're occupied doing something else and want them within earshot or eye-shot, or when they just want to be near you. The signature trait of both the nook and the mini is that they are integrated into another space—*but they are not the main focus of the space.* And yet, while compact, they're still thoughtful and curated. Our goal is to create a space that is both functional and aesthetically pleasing—and the solution for both of those is to keep clutter to a minimum.

The only difference between the nook and the mini is that the nook has two walls (such as a corner) and the mini has one. Other than that, the considerations are the same.

- ▶ **Selecting toys:** Ask yourself these two main questions: *What toys should be there,* and *How will they be displayed?*

- ▶ **Organizing:** Cubby-style organizers are ideal for both of these spaces, because they naturally limit the toys to a reasonable number.

- ▶ **Optimizing:** Vertical organizers and play tables are great for getting the most out of your space in a nook, which is also helpful if you have kids of varying ages and want to separate their things.

- ▶ **Making it part of your home:** Remember that this is part of your adult-use home. Feel free to blend the color and style of your organizers with your decor.

- ▶ **Keeping things visible:** Decorative baskets and cubes that conceal what's inside are still a no-no. The same play-inspiring rules apply here. (See page 75 for a refresher.)

- ▶ **Choosing a location:** Set up a nook or mini in rooms where you tend to spend the most time. If your home has multiple floors, consider having at least one on each.

- ▶ **Keeping it safe:** Skip the kitchen if you can. It's not where you want kids underfoot, especially if space is tight. Ideally the closest nook or mini would be in an adjacent room.

Troubleshooting Communal Spaces

When I first asked the Mothercould community what questions they had about organizing their kids' toys, a majority of the thousands of responses I received were some variation of, "How do I make it feel like my kids' toys aren't taking over my entire house?" If you've made it this far, you know that a big part of the solution is to have fewer toys out for your child to play with. That's a win-win: more play for them and less stuff for your living room. But . . . we're still talking about toys here, and there is a law in physics about how our children's stuff will always end up taking over in the end. Okay, I'm exaggerating, but I get it—even Marc and I find ourselves trying to figure out why Saturday afternoons somehow involve our entire living room becoming buried under a pile of princess dresses and wigs. Luckily, there are solutions!

When Toys Travel

Play hot spots are not just more places to stick toys as you come across them, and your nooks and minis will only stay functional if they follow the play-space-organizing guidelines. The natural law of toys is that they will never stay in one place. They often travel from room to room, until they get deposited in the middle of the floor, stairs, kitchen counter, or all of the above. But instead of stuffing those items into toy storage wherever you find them, you'll want to get into the habit—or better yet, teach your child the habit—of putting things back where they go.

When Toys Are Enormous

You know the ones—the dream houses, the garages, the work-benches, the train tables. The toys that took all of winter break to build and are now another piece of furniture in your house. If these large items are no longer getting the attention they once did, this section may not ultimately be for you, because that thing should be heading to its next home—and not staying in yours. But if the large toy is still in use, that's another story.

Large toys are a unique challenge because they take up a lot of room—often more room than you'd like to have dedicated to play, especially in the middle of your living room. The first thing to do is to consider this item as its own piece of furniture and use it as part of your play-space decor. Make it the focal point of that play zone, maybe tying in shelves or cubbies around it to encourage related open-ended play. Another helpful solution is to use the item itself for storage as best you can, and in a way that doesn't limit your child's ability to play with that item. For example, you could keep doll accessories in zip-top pouches, which you can neatly tuck inside a room of a dollhouse.

But the most effective solution for oversized toys is to embrace them. Accept that this is the beautiful, chaotic season of life you're in. Take it as validation that you knocked it out of the park with that gigantic toy your child loves so much. One day, that thing is going to be in the donation pile, and your child will want to know why you're the one crying over it. So for now, let it go!

Nook of the . . .

Kitchen

Living room

Hallway

Portable Play Ideas

THE MAGIC BOX

This is your playtime Hail Mary. It's what you reach for when that important call comes in just as your child is getting tired of playing on their own. It's the chaos-in-the-kitchen calmer. It's the tantrum redirector.

The Magic Box isn't as thoughtfully curated as the Mini (page 125), the Play Tray (page 174), or the On-the-Go (page 183). In fact, it's not curated at all, but it's effective as a short burst of play. It's essentially a bunch of fun odds and ends tossed into a shoebox, basket, reusable zip-top bag, or the like. It also makes cleaning out your toys a little more painless, because you don't have to toss figurines, knickknacks, or pieces from play sets.

Magic Box Bonus: The figurines you collect for your Magic Box can also come in handy for open-ended play on days when you have a little more bandwidth. Bury them in rice or jelly blocks for your child to excavate; add them to a small container, cover with water, and freeze for your child to rescue from under the ice with toy hammers; or toss them in a bathtub and add bubble bath or dark food coloring so you can no longer see the bottom. (Don't worry; it shouldn't stain your tub if you add the water first. Just be aware of any skin sensitivities your child may have before adding anything to their bath.) For an easy sensory activity, have your child stick their hands in the water and see if they can guess which item they've grabbed.

The **Splash Zone**

CHAPTER 6

T his one goes out to all of you who are not quite sold on bringing potentially messy play into your home. It also goes out to all of you who have ever had an afternoon where the clock seems to be ticking backward while you're running out of ways to keep everyone sane, especially when it's too cold or too inclement to go outside—or to any parent who has ever struggled to get their kid bathed. To all of you I say: Take it to the bathroom.

The bathroom is the most underrated play space in the house. It's already a whole different level of fun to put on a bathing suit, let alone be as creatively free and messy (though stain-free!) as you want to be. Meanwhile, your child is reaping all the benefits of sensory play, but in a contained place where things are meant to get wet. And even the cleanup is fun; just give everyone a squeegee or sponge and let them go to town.

Plus, everyone's bathed, in jammies, and ready for dinner. Seriously, take it to the bathroom!

Depending on the ages of your children, bathroom play may not be as independent as elsewhere in the house, because you'll want to keep an eye on little ones in slippery spaces or in standing water, but these activities are still open-ended and imaginative and working the same important playtime muscles. And as I said earlier, be mindful of any sensitivities your child has before adding anything to their bath. Ultimately, no one knows your child better than you!

> **Be mindful of any sensitivities your child has before adding anything to their bath.**

Setting Up Your Splash Zone

The best bathroom to outfit as your play hot spot is one that has a bath or shower, and that you can reasonably supervise if your child isn't old enough to be in there on their own.

The one big difference between this play space and any other is that you don't need to make the toys accessible all the time. It's okay to make the splash zone invite only, especially because it's ultimately in a functional room that isn't intended for kids to come in and slather foam everywhere at any given moment. Instead, gather your materials for play in a bin or caddy that can be tucked into a closet or sit on a shelf.

Notes on Safety

- Be aware of slipping hazards, and consider installing anti-slip strips where needed.

- If your child cannot sit up on their own, do not fill your bath or splash tray with more than two inches of water.

- Check the water temperature to avoid bathwater burn injuries.

- Make sure bath toys are safe and age appropriate. Be sure to avoid any choking hazards, and remove any toys that are cracked or broken.

- Prevent the growth of hazardous mold inside bath toys by sealing shut any holes that water could get into with hot glue. (They will still float!) If mold is discovered, discard the toy or consider washing it with a bleach-and-water solution.[13]

Make It Your Own

There are seemingly endless possibilities when it comes to bath- or shower-friendly activities. Follow the interests of your child and, as always, your personal tolerance for mess. That said, see if you can stretch yourself a *tiny* bit—none of the materials I recommend will stain or otherwise permanently damage your bathroom. These activities are perfect for a wide range of ages and play interests, but if your child really hates taking a bath or shower, you can also think of these materials as tools for making that experience more enjoyable. It's not unlike putting together a nice tray for yourself to enjoy a luxurious soak with your candle, your book, your glass of wine; all these materials help set the mood in a positive way.

Here are some fun items to add to your splash zone:

- Bath bombs
- Sponges
- Foam letters and numbers
- Squirt bottles
- Paintbrushes
- Bath toys or figurines (Another great way to repurpose odds and ends when you clean everything out initially. Just be sure to cover any holes that water could get into with hot glue, or mold will grow inside.)
- Muffin tin (You can fill each compartment with toys, bath bombs, sponges, etc.)
- Food coloring (I've never met a kid who doesn't want to get into a fun-colored bath. Just be sure to go easy—a couple of drops go a long way!)
- Plastic liquid droppers (These are great for building fine-motor skills.)
- Bath-safe paint and crayons
- Shaving cream or whipped cream paint (page 146)
- Rescue pucks (page 146)
- Play foam (page 169)

Activities for the Splash Zone
(Or Other Splash-Friendly Play Spaces)

Color-Building Bath

This activity sounds messier than it is. With just a few easy steps, you can transform bath time into playtime with very little cleanup required.

1. Fill a bathtub or smaller tub you set inside your shower about halfway. (You don't want too much water, because then it will take forever to take on color.)

2. Add a few drops of food coloring to at least two squirt bottles (but up to as many as you like; recycled bottles work well for this too), fill with water, and shake well. Repeat with any additional squirt bottles.

3. Have your child squeeze the first color into the water to see what happens. Add the second color and do the same. Repeat with any remaining colors, seeing how each color interacts with the others. (Don't worry; the coloring won't dye the bath, kids, or bathing suits—and on the off chance it does, you can easily clean it with any bathroom cleaner.)

4. Take the opportunity to talk about colors, temperature, and water movement.

Water Rescue

Place figurines (people, creatures, or animals) in each well of a muffin tin. Fill each well with water (just enough to cover the figurine), add a drop of food coloring, and freeze until solid. Drop the "pucks" into the bath and watch as the colors mix while little ones work to free everyone from the ice.

Shaving Cream Paint

Mix shaving cream with a couple of pumps of shower gel and a tiny drop of food coloring to create instant bath- or shower-friendly paint. I like doing this in the wells of a muffin tin to create a "painter's palette" for my kids. You could also use whipped cream plus food coloring for a taste-safe option. Let your child paint the bath, tile, and themselves! It washes off easily, and any bathroom cleaner will eliminate any lingering color from the grout.

Infant Water Pond

Simply fill a deep tray—like a large rectangular casserole or baking dish—halfway with water, add some rubber ducks or other floating toys, and let your precrawler enjoy dipping their hands and feet, or just splashing the water.

What If Something Stains?

If you have white grout and are using food coloring for your play, there's a chance that it will discolor. But the beauty of the bathroom is that most surfaces, including grout lines, are formulated so you can use just about any bathroom-designed cleaner to bring things back to their original bright white. If you're concerned about this, consider testing on a small area in a place that won't be noticed, to see how that turns out.

Recipe

Ice Paint

You read that right! This colorful craft is fun for kids of all ages. It's especially perfect for the splash zone because your entire shower or bath is essentially your child's canvas, but this activity is just as fun on paper. Whenever you pull this one out, know that you're strengthening your child's hand-eye coordination, creative development, and investment in the creative process of making art versus being attached to the final product. Plus, they'll get a little extra sensory stimulation from the cold. And yes, your child will most likely spend a good amount of time licking these like Popsicles. I can't blame them; they look *tasty*! But don't worry; they're completely taste-safe.

What You'll Need

Ice cube tray

Water

Food coloring

Ice-pop sticks, cut in half

Watercolor paper (If they're not painting in the Splash Zone, I recommend watercolor paper because it's more absorbent than regular paper and won't fall apart from all the moisture. You can find it in your nearest craft store, as well as major retail and department stores.)

Recipe continued on next page.

Instructions

1. Fill the wells of the ice cube tray with water until they are slightly less than full.

2. Add a small drop of the food coloring in each well. Create as many different colors as you like. I love making mine rainbow-colored.

3. Use the flat edge of an ice-pop stick to mix each well, then leave a stick in each well and freeze overnight, with the rounded end sticking out for a smooth handle.

4. Unmold the cubes and use the sticks as handles to paint!

   Note: Because ice can be a choking hazard, be sure to make this a supervised activity if you have little ones.

Bath time

Balcony time

Yard time

CHAPTER 7

The Fresh-Air
Play Space

When most people think of an outdoor play space, they usually picture a big backyard, maybe a swing set or trampoline, possibly a pool, and many, many, *many* requests of "Push me higher!" or "Watch this!" The thing is, *none* of these amenities are required, and just because your child is outside does not mean that independent play goes out the window. (Or I guess technically it does, but you know what I mean.)

I strongly encourage parents to set up a play area outside, because no matter how limited your space may be—whether it's a balcony, a small patio, or a narrow yard—bringing activities outdoors is hugely beneficial for your child . . . and you. For a start, spending time in the fresh air and sunshine can reduce stress levels, regulate hyperactivity, increase serotonin (the feel-good hormone), strengthen the immune system, and improve sleep.[14] It's also really good for the spirit. Think back to your own childhood, when you were shooed outside and told to *just go play*. Most likely, after you spent the first five minutes complaining that you were bored, it opened up a whole new realm of creativity and exploration. There were mud pies and forts and bugs in jars and chalk masterpieces. Sure, it was just one more place to do some of the activities that you'd otherwise choose to do inside. But chances were that it was also the one place where you could be two very important things: messy and loud! Maybe not rolling around in the mud, splatter painting your patio, or screaming into your next-door neighbor's windows, but definitely living a little more wild and a lot more free.

So you can understand why kids love having a space to themselves that's stocked with their favorite play-inspiring toys and activities, including materials that they may not always have a chance to play with when they're indoors, like paint, kinetic sand, playdough, and water. As far as we parents are concerned, it's a win-win; we know our kids are learning skills that translate to real-life solutions, strengthening neural pathways, and practicing fine- and gross-motor skills, but to them, they're just having a blast letting loose and feeling free.

> We know our kids are learning skills that translate to real-life solutions.

Top Questions to Ask Yourself Before Setting Up an Outdoor Space

- ▶ How can I make it safe for independent play?
- ▶ Can an adult comfortably supervise the space from inside, or do they need to be outside?
- ▶ How much can I reasonably store outside—and where?
- ▶ What am I often bringing from the inside that I could just leave outside?
- ▶ What ages do I need to accommodate?
- ▶ What are my child's primary interests?

Find Your Ideal Space

Regardless of its size, your outdoor play space should:

- ▶ be somewhere safe for kids to explore, be physically engaging, and make noise;
- ▶ have a washable surface, such as concrete, tile, grass, or turf;
- ▶ ideally have access to running water or a hose for easy cleanup. You could also just bring out a bin or bucket of water.

Let's Talk About Safety

My advice for keeping kids safe when they're playing outside is the same as when they're playing inside: It all comes back to setting them up for success. Their play area should have appropriate playthings, intuitive storage, and clear physical boundaries, as well as firmly communicated and understood boundaries of other types, if you have older kids. Be sure they know your expectations in terms of where they can play and what they can play with, especially when it comes to things like rocks, plants, trees, mulch, animals, and other elements unique to the outdoors. (For a boundary-setting refresher, flip back to page 36.)

Outside play also requires a dose of common sense: Young children on a balcony or in a fenceless yard will obviously require more supervision than older children in any sort of space. Follow your instincts and your comfort level.

Choose Your Storage Building Blocks

The biggest challenges for an outdoor play area are organization and maintaining a clean space with play tools. I recommend using a portion of your space for one or a couple of these basic storage solutions, which can be purchased in various sizes.

Outdoor storage chest with a lid

These are great for corralling larger toys, such as balls, outdoor game components, and obstacle-course materials, while keeping them clean and mostly dry.

Outdoor shelving

This will be a space saver because you can create vertical storage. It's where you can organize activities and materials, such as shovels, bubbles, jump ropes, finger paint, and toy cars and trucks. Any of the recommended plastic organizers on page 210 are perfect for keeping these items contained and easy to see.

Wall-mounted hooks

If you have a garage, consider adding these to keep larger gross-motor items, such as bicycles, scooters, Hula-Hoops, obstacle-course components, or sports equipment, neatly tucked away.

Scooping, Pouring, and Transferring

One of the biggest reasons I love having a play space outside is because of the many valuable skills kids learn through water play—especially those that make their parents' lives a touch easier. When little ones get in reps of the three main water-play actions—scooping, pouring, and transferring—it directly translates into real-life applications. In particular, this hand-eye coordination shows up at mealtime when pouring their own drinks and using utensils, especially a spoon. And because they get to test their boundaries while playing with spoons and spouted cups outside, they don't have the urge to turn the dinner table into their own personal water table. Beyond that, squirting, stirring, squeezing, and all the other fun things kid-dos get to do when there's a big ole tub of water around are also amazing for developing essential fine-motor skills.[15] See page 163 for all my favorite water-play materials.

Make It Your Own

If you've already completed the steps in part 1 and taken stock of the things you want to include in your space, now you'll have a good idea of what materials, tools, or furniture will help round out the outdoor play area and make it perfectly suited for everyone using it. Below are suggestions to help you get inspired. Start by looking around your house for them; you'd be surprised by how many of these items you already own.

For Keeping It Clean

- A washable surface to put on the ground for kids to sit comfortably can also be used as a clean surface for their paper when drawing or painting, or to keep your outdoor surfaces paint- and marker-free. If doing a dry activity, this could be a bedsheet, towel, shower curtain, or drop cloth. For wet, stick with something absorbent like a towel or even a doggy pad.

- Spray bottles for wiping down dirtied surfaces are a great way for putting little hands to work.

- Painter's tape is the perfect no-mess all-purpose material. Use it for hopscotch, creating a tennis court, jumping squares, or creating a "do not pass Go" visual boundary.

- Sponges do double duty for water play.

For Getting Wet

▶ Large plastic tubs to fill with water offer endless possibilities because kids love scooping and pouring, especially when you add food coloring, ice, and/or water-friendly toys.

▶ Buckets, pitchers, spouted cups

▶ Spoons

▶ Funnels

▶ Scoops or ladles

▶ Kitchen strainer

▶ Sprinklers

▶ Water balloons

▶ Pop-up pool

▶ Food coloring

▶ Play foam (page 169)

For Staying Dry

- ▶ Sand table or sandbox, plus cups, shovels, buckets, or assorted beach toys

- ▶ Rice or beans

- ▶ Kinetic sand

- ▶ Pop-up pool for setting beneath your table to catch any kinetic sand, rice, or beans, so you can easily retrieve them and reuse them over and over. You could also use a drop cloth, shower curtain, towel, or bedsheet.

- ▶ Playdough

- ▶ Finger paint

- ▶ Edible sand (visit mothercould.com for this recipe and others)

- ▶ Taste-safe dirt (visit mothercould.com for this recipe and others)

- ▶ Taste-safe mud (okay, maybe not dry-dry play, but definitely outdoor approved; visit mothercould.com for this recipe and others)

- ▶ Kitchen strainer

- ▶ Measuring cups

For Fine-Motor Play

- ▶ Tongs or scissor scoops
- ▶ Tweezers
- ▶ Measuring cups and plastic cups
- ▶ Chalk
- ▶ Crayons and washable markers
- ▶ Window-safe markers
- ▶ Paintbrushes
- ▶ Spoons
- ▶ Kid-safe knives

For Gross-Motor Play

- ▶ Colorful sports cones
- ▶ Hula-Hoops
- ▶ Jump ropes
- ▶ Sports equipment like balls, bats, bases, and goals
- ▶ Large "hopper" bouncy jumping balls
- ▶ Push cars
- ▶ Bikes, scooters, skates, and safety equipment like helmets and knee and elbow pads

For a Personal Touch

There's no easier way to make a play space feel engaging than to add some of your child's existing toys, especially those that are destined to end up in the giveaway or donation bins from your indoor clean-outs. It's the perfect way to theme your child's play and incorporate their favorite types of toys into outdoor activities. Suddenly "splash in the water" transforms into "Ariel's birthday party!" or "Zuma's rescue mission!" Just remember to set the boundary with your child: Once a toy is an outdoor toy, its home is outside.

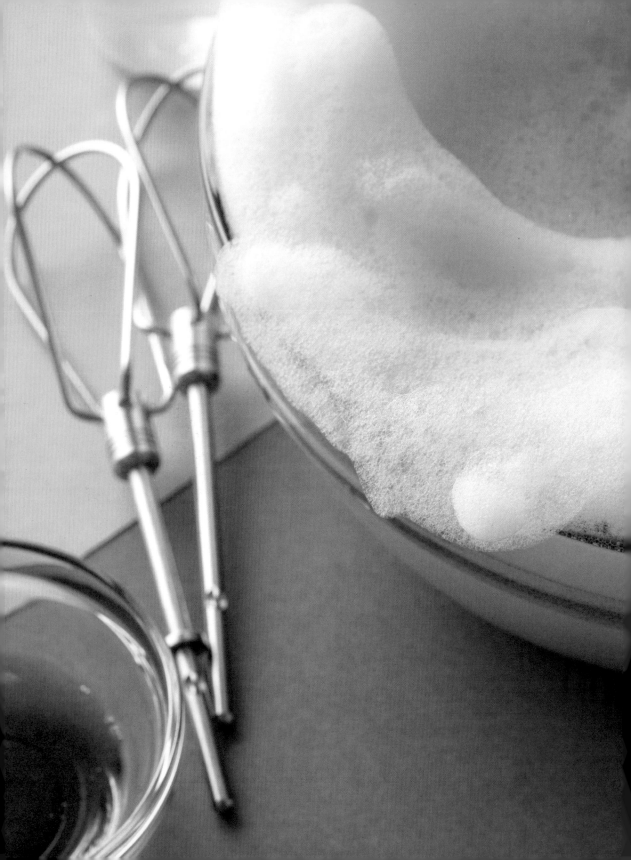

Recipe

Play Foam

It doesn't matter that I'm a thirtysomething adult. Whenever I see a tray of this fluffy, happy-looking foam, I want to dive in headfirst. With just soap, water, and food coloring, you'll be able to whip up the foundation for foamy fantasy play that also engages the senses. I love making this in my go-to play trays, but you could also make the foam in a blender or large bowl and transfer it to your water-play table or a bucket. Or for a wonderfully over-the-top effect, layer multiple batches of different colors in a large, clear plastic tub. But don't save this foam for outdoor play only; it's also great for an indoor activity in the bathroom.

What You'll Need

1 cup water

3 tablespoons tear-free liquid bath soap

2 to 3 drops food coloring

Instructions

1. In a blender, or in a bowl with a hand mixer, combine the water with the soap and food coloring. (The blender will make a smoother foam, while the hand mixer will give you bigger bubbles.)

Recipe continued on next page.

2. Beginning on the lowest speed, increasingly work your way toward high speed until the mixture is frothy and foamy, and holds a stiff peak, 1 to 2 minutes.

3. Enjoy!

For added fun

- ▶ Make blue foam and add sea animals and mermaids for an ocean.

- ▶ Make brown foam, add some cars, and have a car wash.

- ▶ Make green foam and add bugs and flowers for a springtime activity.

- ▶ Make pink foam and add unicorns to let them leap through the clouds.

Fresh Air in the....   Garden

Balcony

Porch

Portable Play Ideas

THE PLAY TRAY AKA PLAYROOM IN A BOX

The Play Tray is a parent's greatest secret weapon. (Well, one of them.) It's what I reach for whenever we have a sitter coming over, or when relatives are visiting who want to spend time with the kids, or when I want to bring something to a family with a new baby. It's essentially the perfect blend of the On-the-Go play space (page 183) and the Magic Box (page 136), because it's a thoughtful selection of toys and activities that's meant to be mobile, as well as have the *wow* factor of playthings that your child doesn't see all the time. It's also perfect for keeping kids entertained when an adult who doesn't normally spend time in the home is there, because they don't have to go searching for scissors or markers, and they don't need to be overly creative with how to prompt play. Instead, the Play Tray provides everything your child needs to complete an activity or set of activities.

I particularly like incorporating a sensory material into these trays because of how endless the play scenarios can be when paired with tools and trinkets. Then I'll pack everything up in a plastic bin where the lid and the container can double as the play surface. This makes for easier mess containment and cleaning up. You can also go with a smaller version to make this portable and toss one in your diaper bag or in the car, or take it with you to restaurants.

My go-to formula for a Play Tray includes:

> **Sensory base material** (such as playdough, dyed rice, or kinetic sand)
>
> **Add a tool** (such as tongs, little scoops, or a funnel, to help with fine-motor skills)
>
> **Add something to make it fun** (Follow your child's interests and go with a theme, or include small figurines or other trinkets from their favorite play sets.)

Play Tray Examples

The Off-Roading Adventure

Sensory base: kinetic sand

Add tools: tongs and spoons

Add something fun: monster trucks, track pieces, figurines

Fun at the Farm

Sensory base: rice

Add tools: scoops and tongs

Add something fun: farm animal figurines and craft-stick "fence posts"

Rainbow Ice-Cream Shop

Sensory base: playdough

Add tools: scoops and cookie cutters

Add something fun: toy ice-cream cones, bowls, colored pom-poms

Recipe
Playdough

This is a Mothercould classic that continues to be one of the most popular. You can customize your own colors, you know exactly what's in it, it's taste-safe, and it lasts for six months when stored in an airtight container at room temperature.

What You'll Need

1 cup all-purpose flour (compacted), plus more as needed

½ cup table salt

2 tablespoons cream of tartar

1 tablespoon oil, such as vegetable or olive oil

Food coloring

1 cup boiling water

Instructions

1. In a large bowl, mix the flour, salt, cream of tartar, and oil.

2. In a measuring cup or small bowl, stir a few drops of food coloring into the boiling water.

3. Add the water mixture to the flour mixture and mix well. Turn out the mixture onto a clean surface and knead until the playdough is no longer sticky. Allow the playdough to cool completely before enclosing it in plastic wrap and storing in an airtight container.
   Tip: If the dough is too sticky, add more flour. If it's too dry, add more water.

CHAPTER 8

The On-the-Go
Play Space

I
t's one thing for your child to entertain themselves at home, where they're surrounded by their usual toys and activities. If they get bored, they usually know how to deal with that. But what about when you leave the house? The doctor's office waiting room, the restaurant, the airport, the car, the religious service—what happens when they have no idea how to deal with those antsy feelings, and you very much need them to be occupied?

That's when you give yourself—and yes, your child—the gift of an on-the-go play space.

This concept is certainly not a new idea; we've been cramming diaper bags full of toys since our kids were born. But we can continue reinforcing independent play and the idea that children are the architects of their entertainment and responsible for their own belongings, even when we're not at home, by being thoughtful about the activities we bring or encourage our kids to pack for themselves.

As our kids get older, it's easy to grab that tablet and call it a day. And while we rely on the screen solution sometimes too, we also mix in other activities. I've found that this keeps everyone less cranky—especially when little eyes and brains get tired or feel motion sickness, but your child doesn't necessarily know how to communicate that—while also keeping them **more** entertained. It's the ultimate antidote to "Are we there yet?!"

Building Your On-the-Go Play Space

▶ Go for activities and toys that are multipurpose, easy to clean up, portable, and lightweight.

▶ Reusable zip-top pouches are great for keeping the pieces of each activity organized, which means less digging through your bag for everything, which means less mess.

▶ When a child is old enough to carry a backpack, around three or four years old, that's when I have them start packing their own bag. (The younger they are, the more gentle oversight they may need.) Packing their bag strengthens their decision-making skills, while also ensuring that they'll have something they're interested in playing with. Sometimes if I see my girls stuffing way too many items in there, I have the knee-jerk reaction of, *We don't need all that stuff!* But if it fits in the backpack and they can carry it, they can take it.

▶ Tuck some cleaning wipes in your travel kit, so you can easily wipe down any overenthusiastic crayon, marker, or playdough marks on travel surfaces. You could also pack a few sheets of plastic wrap to lay over things like airplane trays and restaurant tables. You can fold them up or even just crumple them together, and you'll be able to separate the individual sheets.

▶ Bonus tip: Set expectations. With any toys or activities in any play space, it's important to communicate to your child what's appropriate and what's not. Especially for sensory Play Trays, let your child know that if they're having a hard time keeping the materials on the play surface, it's going to go away until they get another chance to try it again. It might take a few tries to get over the exciting novelty of throwing handfuls of kinetic sand on the floor, but after two or three exposures, they might get the hang of it. Or there's a chance that activities with small or potentially messy pieces might not be the right fit for your child, in which case there are *plenty* of other options (just see the following). Ultimately, the name of the game is setting up both you and your child for success.

Fun for Everyone

- ▶ Playdough Play Tray (page 179)
- ▶ Kinetic sand Play Tray (page 176)
- ▶ The Snack Box (page 190)
- ▶ Paint-with-water coloring books

Winners for Ages Two and Under

- ▶ Foam stickers (great for sticking on—and removing from—restaurant tables, airplane windows, or paper.)
- ▶ Window-cling stickers
- ▶ Fidget toys (I love suction-cup spinners.)
- ▶ Suction-cup "blocks"
- ▶ Cleaning wipes (Kids love to help wipe down their area on a plane.)
- ▶ Play scarves

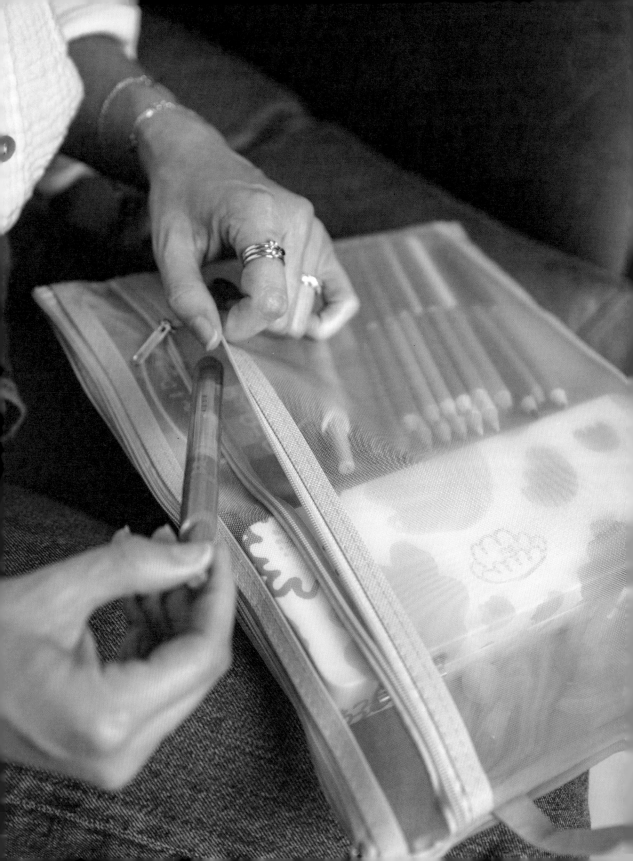

Winners for Older Kids

- ▶ Magnetic puzzles

- ▶ Window-cling stickers

- ▶ Color-by-number activity books—or better yet, the versions that use stickers instead of markers

- ▶ Printable activity packs—check out our Mothercould Printable Activity Packs that can be found within our digital resource *Mothercould in Your Pocket.*[16]

- ▶ Coloring books with twistable crayons. These are preferable to colored pencils or crayons, which will break, or markers, which will end up on an airplane wall.

- ▶ Watercolor paints. Instead of dipping the brushes in water—and risking spills and drips— use a small spray bottle to spritz the paints with a small amount of water.

- ▶ Lanyards and string for making jewelry and key chains or for playing cat's cradle

- ▶ Wipeable drawing tablets or doodle boards

- ▶ Digital cameras

- ▶ Wax craft sticks

The Snack Box

Snacks can be entertainment too! They can also offer a child some independence, instead of needing Mom or Dad to be the official holder of the snacks and opener of the bags. I like to pack a hard-sided, partitioned container for each kid with a wide variety of snacks. That way, they can graze whenever they feel hungry (or bored) and rarely ask for any other options. Then they can tuck it right back into their backpack and continue playing. In fact, it's such an effective snack-activity-hybrid solution that I ended up designing my own Mothercould version! For me, the ideal snack box has removable partitions, so you can make the box fit the snack and not the snack fit the box, and is made of food-grade, microwave-safe, and dishwasher-safe material.

You're going for independence, not a yogurt-covered toddler.

As for what to pack, my rules of thumb are: nothing too juicy or messy (you're going for independence, not a yogurt-covered toddler), nothing that needs to be unwrapped, nothing that needs to be refrigerated (if you're going to be away from the house for a while), and lots of variety.

You'll want to select things based on your child's age, abilities, and preferences. Here are some of my favorite snack-box staples.

- Dried fruit
- Fresh fruit (particularly less-juicy varieties, such as berries, grapes, sliced apples, and clementine segments)
- Veggies (baby carrots, grape tomatoes, sliced celery, sliced bell peppers, and sliced cucumbers)
- Fruit snacks
- Cereal

- Nuts
- Pretzels
- Graham crackers
- Animal crackers
- Chips
- Puffs
- Hard-boiled eggs
- Cheese sticks or mini wheels
- Jerky

Sensory Table in a Box

Depending on where you're going to be and whether you have access to a table, this little kit can be the perfect attention-occupier for your child. It's essentially the Play Tray in miniature. And much like the Play Tray, the basics are:

- ▶ Sensory base material
- ▶ Add tools and accessories
- ▶ Add something to make it fun

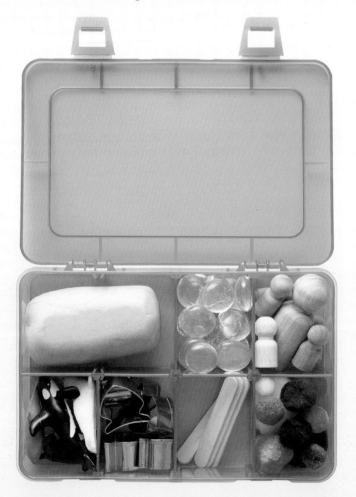

Easy-access bins

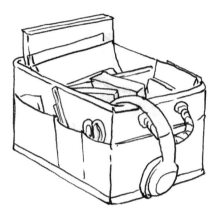

Car organizer

Kids' backpack

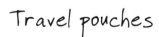

Travel pouches

CHAPTER 9

A Pep Talk for
Independent Play

I f you've made it this far, congratulations! You are already well on your way to a brand-new relationship with play in your household. I know that for some of you, these new systems might feel overwhelming. Change is hard! Heck, finding the time to even make change in the first place is hard! Just remember: None of this needs to happen overnight, and every step you take toward setting up your child for independent play goes a long way, both for you and for them. Even if it's spending one day a week cleaning out your toy collection, even if it's setting aside one weekend to tackle one room at a time over the course of months, even if it's focusing on setting up one small play area at a time—you'll be making your way toward the ultimate goal of less overwhelm for you *and* your child, better-quality play, more creativity for the whole family, and a greater sense of ease in your home. No more struggling to find a place for all your things, no more struggling to inspire your child to help themselves to their own activities, and no more struggling with the thought of, *What else can I buy to keep these kids entertained?*

Throughout this process, be patient with yourself and with your child. Know that just like anything else worth doing, consistency is key. Especially if your child is used to coming home from school and jumping onto their tablet or playing with an adult at all times, and especially if for the past few years the only system in place has been "fill another bin with toys and stash it somewhere." Zero judgment. That's the program in most households.

The transition to creating clearly defined play spaces and independently playing within them will take time. But the journey *is* the destination! The more you model the behavior that you want to see, such as regularly decluttering and taking a thoughtful interest in the toys and activities available so that they're well suited for your child, the more your child can follow your lead. And not only that, but you'll become more tuned in to their interests and how they like to play, which is a parenting win any day. Ultimately, it will become a very satisfying cycle. The more you keep up your end of the bargain, the more incentivized your child will be to take advantage of these new systems. The more they take advantage of these new systems, the more satisfying it is to maintain them. And maybe most importantly, the more you maintain them, the less work it ultimately is to keep things tidy, organized, and play inspiring.

So go ahead: Gift yourself and your family this peace of mind. Take the leap of faith that this will work for you. This is your Mother**could** moment. Because I know you can.

Keep **Playing!**

CHAPTER 10

Storage Solutions

Consider this your go-to resource for all things organization. To make this section as useful as possible, I've divided it into two parts: a glossary of organization from a storage-first perspective (for when you're taking inventory of which types of storage you already own), and a glossary of organization from an activity-first perspective (for when you need to figure out how best to corral a certain type of toy or play). Eventually, you'll start to see the patterns of how things are best organized. It will also be helpful to revisit these lists again and again as your child's play spaces change and their play evolves. It's just one more way for me to support you every step of the way.

My Favorite Storage Systems

Open shelving

This type of storage, whether you're using individual shelves or bookcases, is the foundation of most of my play spaces. They're easier to keep clutter-free than closed storage (they truly keep you honest), you can see everything you have, and they're accessible. You can either set your toys directly on the shelf, or you can arrange your baskets and bins on there. Either way, your child can see exactly where everything is—and where it goes when playtime is over.

You also get great vertical storage with shelving, which allows you to maximize the space you have. A great way to take advantage of that height is to place older children's toys on the higher shelves, while keeping items for little ones below. Shelves that aren't reachable by any child can be used for storage as well. My biggest recommendation for these types of shelves is to go with solid shelving versus slatted, so smaller items don't fall through. That said, you can use shelf liners to help prevent things from slipping through the cracks.

A subset of open shelving is cubby storage, which I really love. That's because you can use this easy-to-follow rule: one item or one activity per cube. Plus, you can stack a few (*just a few!*) things on top.

If you're not completely sold on open shelving, one exception I'd make in this category is for a freestanding closet with doors, that has open shelving inside.

Great for

Magnetic tiles, wooden blocks, baby toys, stacking toys, freestanding toys, books (stacked or slotted into a wooden dish rack), and anything else stored in a clear or wire bin.

Wall storage

This is another great way to create more vertical storage, while also turning your toys into decor. Think knobs or hooks (especially for dress-up clothing), pegboards, bulletin boards, magnetic boards, and "specialty" items, such as decorative storage for collections. If you're using knobs or hooks for dress-up clothing, consider

hanging one lower to the ground and one slightly higher, to utilize as much wall space as possible and double your real estate.

Great for

Dress-up or imaginative play, tools, books, building creations, arts and crafts displays, toy cars, and figurines.

Clothing racks

These "fashion" racks are super handy for hanging up clothing for imaginative play. Coat racks would also work well for this, as long as there's no risk of little ones pulling them over.

Shallow bins

The essential ingredient for keeping your play space clutter-free. Bins help keep like items together without being so large that you can't see what's in them at first glance, which offers the best insurance against your child dumping things out all over the floor. You can find bins in a variety of sizes, and they can either be clear or colorful, depending on your preference. The key to a bin's success is to not cram too much in there. Consider using one bin for one activity. Or when grouping like activities, such as puzzles, keep it to two to three *max*. You can also use zip cases or zip-top pouches to keep smaller items organized within a larger category.

Bins without lids can be either stand-alone bins that sit on a shelf or in a cubby, or they can be drawer-style bins, such as the IKEA TROFAST system—the only type of drawer I approve of in a play space. That's because you can still see inside, even when it's closed (or you can label the outside), and it's usually not so deep (ideally no more than four to six inches) that the contents become a jumble.

Lidded bins, especially ones that are clear, are perfect for out-of-rotation toy storage because they are stackable or can be slid under beds or perched up high on closet shelves.

Great for

Small dolls and accessories, sensory activities, multiple-piece sets, wooden blocks, puzzles, and games.

Trays

The beauty of a tray is that it's not only toy storage, but it's also a play surface. When I use trays in my kids' play spaces, it's a way for me to indicate that "everything here goes together." The ideal trays have shallow sides and are about two inches deep.

Great for

    Sensory activities (see the Play Tray on page 174), arts and crafts activities, board games (you can put the pieces directly on the tray), a doll and its accessories, blocks, and small play sets.

Cubes

    Similar to bins, these are great for holding all the pieces of one certain type of toy, and they look particularly great when popped into cube storage. Either go for see-through (clear or colorful) plastic or wire that you can see through. I like the ones that have a little bit of a dip in front, so little hands can reach inside.

Great for

    Balls, stuffies, blocks, and small play sets.

Baskets

    When it comes to certain types of toys—particularly larger toys—you have my permission to use storage that you can't see through. Although, I'd argue that this type of storage is most successful when it's short enough that you can see at least some of what is inside, or, if it's more than six inches deep, when it has a wide enough weave that you can see straight through it. But yes, I will grant you that baskets can look really nice; you just have to be strategic in how you use them. I particularly like soft-sided baskets for the floor to hold items for babies and toddlers. Baskets with handles are also great if you have items that would be handy in another play space from time to time. Just no lids! That's an order.

Great for

Board books, balls, stuffies, soft accessories like baby-doll bibs and blankets, and play scarves.

Trading card books

These books that you can buy online contain sleeves for things like playing cards, cars, small dolls, and stickers. They're great for older children who have collections and are interested in taking a little more pride in or care of their items.

Hard-sided zip cases and zip-top pouches

Okay, *these* might be my very favorite organizational tool. They are perfect for corralling items within a larger category. Say, for example, your child's enormous toy-car collection. They could all go into a bin, and you can use cases or pouches to sort them into categories, such as monster trucks, emergency vehicles, and race cars. Or you can have a bin dedicated to dolls and use a pouch or a case for each doll to keep their clothes and accessories separate. These are also amazing for storing game or puzzle pieces without needing to keep the box (a great space saver). Plus, when it comes time to pack for a trip or an outing, you only need to grab a few of these pouches or cases and be on your way.

Great for

Everything. Cars, small blocks, puzzles, games, dolls, and imaginative play accessories.

Snack boxes

Specifically hard-sided boxes with compartments. There is no accessory too small for this workhorse of an organizer. If your boxes have removable dividers, you could also make room to store a larger toy with its accessories.

Great for

Doll accessories, trinkets, hair accessories, jewelry, beads, play coins, small LEGO bricks, and magnetic play sets.

String

Maybe the most underrated storage tool! Hang a string (securely and out of reach, so it's not a choking hazard) in your play space, and you can use clips or clothespins to create instant art displays and storage. Use them for your play scarves, finished art pieces (especially if they need to air-dry), or doll dresses. Simply tie the string to something sturdy—high enough so little ones can't grab it—or use adhesive wall hooks.

Caddies and lazy Susans

These are perfect for turning any table into a creation station.

Great for

Arts and crafts, sensory play, and science experiments.

Wooden dish rack

This is my favorite way to display books on a shelf.

Tiered rolling cart

This is pretty much the perfect play-space addition. It has a small footprint, is portable, and can accommodate an entire station for play.

Great for

Arts and crafts, sensory play, LEGO bricks, blocks, magnetic tiles, and books. See organization ideas on page 112.

Book rails

I love a book wall made up of book rails because of the instant warmth it adds to a space, with very little investment. Book rails are also another great way to take advantage of vertical space. And the beauty of a book rail versus a bookshelf is that you're innately limited to a handful of books, while also getting to see their beautiful covers.

Storage to Avoid

Cubbies with large baskets or bins you can't see through

These are a little *too* good at hiding clutter. They easily become dumping grounds for toys, so they get over-stuffed. And because you can't see what's inside, they're prime targets for dump-and-runs.

Boxes or baskets with lids

When storage containers "click" shut, your child will most likely not be able to open them. You want them to be able to freely grab their toys, and not have to run to you for help every time they want to play. And anything that keeps you from being able to see inside, no matter how organized you are, will lead to forgotten playthings.

For more information and links to some
of my favorite storage products, go to
www.mothercould.com

This could also look like . . .

this.

Toy Storage
Glossary

By Activity

Arts and crafts

Separate all materials into their own bins, caddies, pouches, or cases. These can then be stored inside a bin, drawer, arts and crafts table, or tiered cart. Alternatively, use a partitioned lazy Susan, placing each type of material in each section.

Blocks and building

Your storage choice will depend on the type and size of your blocks or toys for building. For larger wooden blocks or magnetic tiles, clear bins or cubes are great, especially if they have a slightly open front for easy grabbing. I like sorting my magnetic tiles by color, which makes them look extra enticing. I'll also set out the booklet with building "recipes" that comes with the blocks, offering another alluring invitation for play.

If your blocks can be stacked, such as Montessori-style wooden blocks, these can be set on a shelf, in their own cubby, or in a tray—and make really nice decorations.

For smaller blocks, such as LEGO bricks, you have a few options. Some children like keeping the sets together, which you can easily do in a storage bag, pouch, or case (ditch the box and be sure to save the instructions!). For the children who want more free-form building, you can sort the blocks by shape or color. Snack boxes work well, as do small bins, especially when they're arranged on a tiered cart. Or, if LEGO is really your child's thing, consider investing in a LEGO table with built-in storage.

Books

Stack in a small basket on the floor (for board books), on a wooden dish rack, on book racks and ledges, or on the tiers of a cart. Be sure to pair books with a comfy place to read, such as a plush area rug or beanbag chair.

Cars and vehicles

If it's a sizable collection, bins get the job done, potentially with smaller bins, cases, or pouches inside to organize the cars into categories. If your child has favorites, these can be displayed on a shelf or tray or set aside in a collectibles book. Track pieces can be disassembled and held in bins or baskets.

Dolls

You have a few storage options here, and they mostly depend on the size of your dolls. Larger dolls can be collected in clear deeper bins, cubes, or baskets. Accessories can be sorted by type (shoes, clothes, activities) or by individual dolls in storage bags or pouches or the compartments of a snack container. Another option is to pack up each individual doll with its accessories in bins, pouches, or zippered cases. This makes it easier to rotate out dolls, especially if your child has a sizable collection. You'd be amazed how "like-new" these dolls feel when they come back out of storage!

Dress-up/imaginative play

I like three storage approaches to clothing. For costumes, I either hang them on hooks or knobs, hang them on a standing rack, or fold them nicely into drawers. (One of the rare times you'll see me using drawers.) That said, the most effective solutions that are the easiest to maintain are, hands down, hooks, knobs, and standing racks. For accessories, I like to separate them into categories, such as gloves, wigs, masks, hats, badges, gear, and jewelry. Shallow drawers are great here, especially if you can add smaller bins, dividers, or compartments in the drawers for the small bits like earrings and necklaces. Shoes can be lined up neatly beneath the clothes, or on top of the drawer system, if you go in that direction.

Games

Stack board games or card games nicely on open shelving (a fun opportunity for color coordinating). Or for a much more efficient use of space, transfer the pieces and components to storage bags or pouches. If you have older kids, you could potentially store your games with the out-of-rotation toys or in a cabinet, in a closet, or under the TV on your console. That's because we've found that board games become a sort of "destination" play—meaning, as you no longer have heaps and heaps of them, kids remember which board games they have, and they tend to be whole-family activities.

Kitchen

This will depend on whether you have a play kitchen; often that piece of furniture comes equipped with its own storage. If you do have a kitchen, look for bins that fit inside all possible "shelves"—especially the oven and fridge. Larger items, especially appliances, can then be set on top or on the counter. Or if you don't have a kitchen—or you need a little extra storage—a cubby system with clear bins or shallow drawers goes a very long way. Storage bags and pouches can also be great for sorting things like utensils, plates, and play food.

Musical instruments

Smaller items can go in shallow bins, drawers, baskets, or trays, while larger items can be displayed right on a shelf.

Play "sprinkles"

These are the assorted items that can enhance other play ingredients. Scarves can be tossed into baskets or bins or clipped onto a string for display. Flashlights can be arranged on a tray or tucked into a zip-top bag. Sensory bottles can be placed directly on a shelf or on top of a play kitchen (they're great as pretend drinks), or collected on a tray or in a basket or bin.

Puzzles

Puzzle racks are great space savers (but I recommend fighting the urge to fill the entire rack at once). I love keeping all the pieces for each puzzle in its own zip-top pouch or storage bag, so pieces don't go missing. Alternatively, you could set puzzles directly on an open shelf or in a cubby, or inside a shallow bin, ideally no more than two to three per bin. If your child loves puzzles and it's a primary attraction in your play space, you can sort them by theme (animals, things that go, fairies).

Screen time and gaming

Devote a shallow drawer or tray to the controllers and any accessories. Be sure to add a comfy chair if there isn't already one in your play space.

Sensory activities and science experiments

Assemble these on trays or in shallow bins (with any sensory materials stored in their own airtight containers, to minimize mess and extend their shelf life). Store with all necessary toys and tools for that activity, for easy grab-and-go playtime.

Sports and gross-motor skills

Baskets and bins are great for balls of pretty much any size. Smaller items such as jump ropes can be tucked into shallow bins, and larger items (scooters, trampolines, balance toys) can be freestanding or set on a low shelf.

Tool bench

Similar to how to handle the kitchen, you'll either maximize your existing tool-bench space with bins and storage bags, or look to extra shelving or shallow drawers. A snack box and storage bags go a long way for all those little nuts and bolts!

Acknowledgments

Writing a book has been the experience of a lifetime, and the reason it has been so rewarding (and happened in the first place!) is because of some very special people:

My husband Marc, who has not only been my partner in love for the past fifteen years, but also my partner in Mothercould. Thank you for being an unwavering believer, my biggest supporter, and my greatest cheerleader. I could not have written this book—or created this beautiful life—without you. Te amo.

My manager, Hilary Williams, who saw the potential in Mothercould and knew that it had the power to touch the lives of so many. You are a role model both personally and professionally and inspire me every day. Thank you for making so many of my dreams come true.

My literary agent, Brandi Bowles, who believed in the impact this resource could have and helped me put all the puzzle pieces together. I'm grateful for your leadership and support in making this book a reality.

My collaborator, Rachel Holtzman, who not only breathed life into my ideas but also provided guidance and perspective throughout the publishing process. You are an incredible writer, but an even better friend. I'm honored to have collaborated with you on this project.

The team at Harper Celebrate, particularly MacKenzie Howard, Sabryna Lugge, Michael Aulisio, and Bonnie Honeycutt, who were unwavering in their support and essential to bringing this beautiful resource to life. Thank you for helping make a positive impact on the lives of so many.

Photographer Kris D'Amico and the Reactor Media team, for the lovely images that not only make the book feel so special but that will also continue to be keepsakes for my family.

Illustrator Mat Edwards, who somehow took all the images in my brain and transformed them into perfect pieces of art that make this book a more helpful resource.

Diandra Escamilla and the team at Align Public Relations for amplifying the reach of this book while helping me stay true to myself and Mothercould.

And last but certainly not least, the Mothercould community. Thank you for so graciously letting me into your lives and sharing your hopes, dreams, fears, and frustrations so that we can all learn and grow together. I started Mothercould because I was yearning for a community like the one we've built together. Thank you for always being there for me and my family with your love and positivity. It means more to us than words can express.

Notes

1   Ralph Moller, "Exploring the Benfits of Sensory Play for Children," Above & Beyond Therapy, abtaba.com, April 10, 2024, https://www.abtaba.com/blog/benefits-of-sensory-play-for-children#:~:text=Fine%20motor%20skills%20involve%20the,small%20muscle%20groups%20%5B2%5D.

2   Nancy Mattia and Fiona Tapp, "Getting Started with Independent Play," *Parents*, September 8, 2022, https://www.parents.com/baby/development/intellectual/the-valueof-solo-play/.

3   Apryl Duncan, "Playing Alone Is Important for Kids—Here's Why," *Parents*, December 15, 2023, https://www.parents.com/playing-alone-8413896.

4   Moller, "Exploring the Benfits of Sensory Play for Children."

5   Becky Harlan and Summer Thomad, "The 5-minute daily playtime ritual that can get your kids to listen better," National Public Radio, NPR.com, updated December 21, 2022, https://www.npr.org/2022/10/13/1128737199/the-5-minute-daily-playtime-ritual-that-can-get-your-kids-to-listen-better.

6   Jocelyn Solis-Moreira, "How Long Does It Really Take to Form a Habit?" *Scientific American*, January 24, 2024, https://www.scientificamerican.com/article/how-long does-it-really-take-to-form-a-habit/.

7   Mattia and Tapp, "Getting Started with Independent Play," *Parents*, https://www.parents.com/baby/development/intellectual/the-value-of-solo-play/#:~:text=At%20 6%20months%2C%20a%20child,should%20last%20around%2030%20minutes.

8   "What Is Sensory Play? The Benefits for Your Child and Sensory Play Ideas," Cleveland Clinic, ClevelandClinic.org, March 18, 2022, https://health.clevelandclinic.org/benefits -of-sensory-play-ideas.

9   "What Is Sensory Play?"

10   "What Is Sensory Play?"

11   "What Is Sensory Play?"

12   Nicole Chevrier, "Slow Down and Boost Your Mental Health," Mental Health Commission of Canada, mentalhealthcommission.ca, August 21, 2023, https://mentalhealthcommission.ca/blog-posts/65262-slow-down-and-boost-your-mental-health/.

13   Shobha Bhaskar, MD, "Mold in Bath Toys," March 16, 2021, ChildrensMD.org, https://childrensmd.org/browse-by-topic/safety/mold-in-bath-toys/.

14   Claire McCarthy, MD, "6 Reasons Children Need to Play Outside," Harvard Health Publishing, Harvard.edu, October 27, 2020, https://www.health.harvard.edu/blog/6-reasons-children-need-to-play-outside-2018052213880.

15   "The Benefits of Water Play for Childhood Development," Busy Bees, busybees.edu.au, October 30, 2020, https://www.busybees.edu.au/the-benefits-of-water-play-for-childhood-development-2/.

16   *Mothercould in Your Pocket*, online resource, www.mothercould.com/mothercould-in-your-pocket.

About the Author

Myriam Sandler is the creator of Mothercould (@mothercould), a kids' activity and family lifestyle platform with a global community of millions of parents, educators, and caregivers. Born in Venezuela and raised in Miami, Florida (where she now resides), the bilingual mother of three shares unique, short video tutorials of sensory and food recipes, parenting hacks, family travel tips, and product recommendations. The visually captivating content throughout social media and branded channels is quick and easy to follow, offering simple and accessible play solutions. This ever-expanding platform has been featured by outlets such as CNBC, Nickelodeon Parents, Good Morning America, Google Web Creators, *The Sun*, Televisa Univision, and Telemundo. Most recently, Myriam has developed problem-solving products for families, with Mothercould offerings on online retailers such as Amazon, Walmart, and Target. Prior to launching Mothercould, Myriam led the women and children's program for the Salvation Army homeless shelter in Miami, where she assisted families as they navigated out of homelessness.

For more about Myriam and Mothercould, visit:

www.mothercould.com

@mothercould on social media